Anthology of Italian and Italo-American Poetry

Anthology of Italian

and

Italo-American Poetry

Translated into English by
RODOLFO PUCELLI

BOSTON
BRUCE HUMPHRIES, INC.
PUBLISHERS

PREFACE

This anthology of Italian and Italo-American poetry is the first of its kind to be published in the United States, and perhaps in both Americas. Apparently the American born did not care to tackle such a hard task, while Americans of Italian birth were for the most part unable to do it. In any case, they had not the constancy and passion that such a task requires.

It was not easy for me to collect in only one hundred and twenty-eight pages sample poems of so great a number and variety of poets, some in translation and some in the original English. Of the classic poets I could have selected many more, and of the living ones too. But it would have required a volume of many more pages. Such a book is not practical today, especially if we consider that many of its purchasers would be working people who are able to buy very few books of poetry. However, it is confidently predicted that this unique anthology will be appreciated and kept in every honest and educated Italo-American home, as a precious gift made possible through the efforts of men who have devoted their best years to literature, languages, criticism, and journalism.

Several Italo-American poets whom I would have liked to include could not be reached, because they are not yet well known; while others hesitated to send in their poems for fear they might be asked to buy some copies. Others, perhaps, had planned translations of their own. Consequently it has not been possible to include any poems of Pasquale De Biasi, Vincenzo Manente, Umberto Liberatore, Enzio Giustiniani, Giuseppe Chiarella, Isidoro Filocco, the late Italo Stanco, Lorenzo Lucarelli, and some others, especially women—all good and deserving the honor of representation in this anthology.

On the other hand, a few—very few—of those included may not be great poets, but they were willing to contribute their poems and to sacrifice, to some extent, their rights of translation and publication. It need not be added that the book, for obvious reasons, does not contain a single poem in the original Italian.

I am glad and honored indeed to have the approval and support of such celebrated poets as Lionello Fiumi, Luigi Fiorentino, Giuseppe Villaroel, Roberto Cervo, Antonio Manuppelli,

Angiolo Orvieto, Claudio Allori, Aldo Capasso, together with some others, all of them poets who enjoy a wide reputation in Italy and abroad and who are the heralds of Italian poetry today.

Among Italo-Americans represented are some who are really very good poets and whose names are known here and also in Italy, the country of their origin.

I thank all those friends who recognized the value of this anthology and who have aided me in my endeavors, trusting in my willingness and ability to carry out this difficult task.

RODOLFO PUCELLI

New York, July, 1954

ITALIAN POETS

Translations by Rodolfo Pucelli

BEYOND THE SPHERE

Beyond the widest sphere there is in space,
Passes a sigh out of my heart's deep gloom;
A new intelligence, which Love's sad doom
Engenders, wings it up in lofty chase.

As soon as it arrives in that high place
Of its desire, it sees a Lady, whom
All honor, and who shines, and for whose bloom
The pilgrim spirit gazes on her face.

It sees in her what, when it speaks to me,
I do not grasp, so subtle its speaking is
To my poor heart, in which it whispers low.

Yet know I whom it speaks of covertly,
For oft recurs the name of Beatrice,
And what it means by that, Ladies, I know.

Dante Alighieri
(1265-1321)

YOU WHO HEAR . . .

O ye who hear in scattered rhymes the sound
Of those deep sighs on which I used to feed
My heart, when I, still young, was not yet rid
Of the light errors that our mind confound;
   For the strange way in which I with profound
Feeling am crying and reasoning amid
Vain hopes and pain, I hope to find the meed
Of pity and pardon by those who are love-bound.
   But well I see now how the laughing-stock
I was for years among the folk; so I am now
Often ashamed and less myself esteem:
   And for my folly are shamefulness and mock
The fruit, and to repent, and clearly know
That what the world likes is a fleeting dream.

Francesco Petrarca
(1304-1374)

NOW THAT THE SKY . . .

Now that the sky, the earth, and breezes are
    Quiet, and beasts and birds are all asleep,
    Night turns her starry chariot, and the deep
    Seems to be waveless near the coast, and far;

I see, muse, burn, and sigh; and like a star
    Love shines before me, and I cannot sleep:
    Yet when I think of her I cease to weep,
    Forgetting all about my inward scar.

Thus only from one vivid source and clear
    Derive the sweet and sour on which I feed,
    And one sole hand heals me and pricks by stealth;

And to keep always my deep sore astir,
    One thousand times I die, and like a seed
    Revive each day, so far I am from health.

                  Francesco Petrarca

SOUL, THAT SO VARIOUS . . .

Soul, that so various and so many things
See, hear and read and speak and think and write,
My eager eyes and ears, that with delight
Celestial words convey to my heart strings:

Oh, would ye not renounce the throne of kings
To have come earlier, or with hair all white,
On this rough path, not to find eyes so bright,
Nor footsteps such as these, that give me wings?

Now with a light so clear, with such a mark,
It would be shame to err on the brief way
That well could lead to heaven out of the dark.

Strive to ascend, my soul, amid the grey
Mist of her anger, following, steady and stark,
Her honorable steps and heavenly ray.

                  Francesco Petrarca

[10]

LOVE THAT SEES ALL THOUGHT OPENLY

O Love, to whom wide open is my thought,
And the hard path on which you lead me, please
Look with your piercing eyes deep into these
My heart's pains known to you, to others not.

To follow you, you know how many I got
Sufferings; yet from hill to hill at ease
You go all day, despising rest and peace
And without taking of my efforts note.

I see, indeed, from far the beacon light
To which you goad and turn me, but I have
No wings like you, to accelerate my flight.

Yet, if I never reach what I so crave
And pine away, alas, out of her sight,
I would be glad to please her, till the grave.

Francesco Petrarca

HE WHO REVEALED . . .

He who revealed in his activity
Infinite providence and wondrous skill,
Who shaped both hemispheres at his own will
And milder Jupiter than Mars: when he

Came to this earth to explain the verity
Of Scripture, full of mystery until
That time, took John and Peter, who were still
Fishing with nets, to heaven gloriously.

As for his birthplace he did not choose Rome
But small Judea; so he liked to grace
Humility above all other things.

So now he gives us from a village home,
This star, and we thank Nature and the place
In which such beauty saw her first life-springs.

Francesco Petrarca

[11]

TO MYSELF

Now you will rest forever, tired heart.
The last illusion, thought eternal, gone,
In both of us: I know the wish has ceased
For dear illusions, and our hope as well.
Rest, rest forever. You have panted long,
Your impulses and motions all in vain.
Nor is it worth your while to sigh for earth.
Bitterness, boredom is our life. The world
Is filth. Now be appeased. For the last time,
Despair. Fate offered to our human kind
One good thing only: death. Now set at naught
Yourself, your nature, and the hideous power
That rules unseen all things for common harm,
The infinite vanity of all earthly things.

Giacomo Leopardi
(1798-1837)

SNOWFALL

Slowly the snow drifts down from the ashen skies.
No sound of life, no more the city's din;
The herb-woman's cry is hushed, the rattling of cars;
No joyous song of love and passionate youth.
From the tower in the square groan through the air the hours
Hoarse as a sigh from a world far off from day.
The wandering birds peck at my frosty panes
Like friendly spirits, watching and calling me.
Soon, very soon, my dear ones—O heart, be calm!—
I come to the silence, I come to my shadowy rest.

Giosue Carducci
(1835-1907)

IN THAT NIGHT

Unlucky he who roaming in that night,
  Pursued and egged by terror at his heels,
  Heard screech owls shrilly call blood-curdling peals
And one lone bitch in loud, long, mournful plight.
Pale ghosts of Erebus did here alight,
  And that malicious thief who robs and steals,
  Detesting light where mountain path reveals,
Did not descend that night because of fright.
Like a dark mass of agitating scurries,
  The witches quickly came down from their slopes
  To sordid rite of devilish hugs till morn.

Unlucky he who mid those frights and worries
    Came to this world; for him are vain all hopes.
    And in that night I was unhappily born!
                              Lorenzo Stecchetti
                                  (1845-1916)

OLIVE SUNDAY
The birds have finished building their nests today.
It is the feast of olives; their fluttering wings
Rest on their work of leaves and twigs and hay.

That on the cypress, this one on the bay,
In woods along a stream that flows and sings,
In shadows moved by golden shiverings.

And they brood on their nests of lichen and moss,
Mutely looking up at the limpid sky,
With sudden palpitation, if across
A bee comes humming, a maybug, or a fly.
                              Giovanni Pascoli
                                  (1865-1912)

STAMPING
A gallop is heard far away
(It is what . . . ?)
It comes nearer, runs on the plain
With tremulous speed.

A desolate, infinite plain;
Ample, arid, and even:
Some shadow of bird gone astray
That glides in the air like an arrow.

Nothing else. They all run away,
Afraid, from some distant destruction:
But which one, or where it may be
Is known not on earth, nor in heaven.

A gallop is heard far away
And louder refrain.
It comes nearer, it runs on the plain:
Ah, death! . . . it is death! it is death!
                              Giovanni Pascoli

RAIN IN THE PINE GROVE

Hush! On the threshold
Of the grove I don't hear
Voices that you call
Human; but I hear
Words that are newer, spoken
By the drops and leaves
Far away.
Listen. It rains
From the scattered clouds.
It rains on the brackish
And sun-burned tamarisks,
It rains on the scaly
And bristly pines,
It rains on the divine
Myrtle-trees,
On the furze, fulgent
And thick with flowers,
On the juniper laden
With fragrant berries;
It rains on our
Sylvan faces;
It rains on our
Gloveless hands,
On our light
Clothing,
On the fresh thoughts
That the renewed soul
Discloses,
On the beautiful fable
That yesterday
Beguiled you, today beguiles me,
Hermione!

Don't you hear? The rain
Falls on the solitary
Verdure
With cracklings that endure
And vary in the air
According to the boughs
More rare, less rare.
Listen! The weeping

Is followed by the song
Of the cicadas
Whom the south wind's cry
Does not scare,
Nor does the ashy sky.
And the pine
Has one sound, and the myrtle
Another sound, and the juniper
Still another, different
Instruments
Under numberless fingers.
And we are both
Immersed in the sylvan
Spirit,
Living a life arboreal
And your raptured features
Are wet with rain
Like a leaf,
And your hair
Is smelling like
The clear furze,
O terrestrial creature
Who are called
Hermione!

Listen, listen! The tune
Of the aerial cicadas
Grows little by little
Duller beneath
The weeping that
Increases;
But a song, hoarser,
Blends with it
Mounting up
From the moist shadow, afar.
Duller and hoarser
It slacks, it goes out.
Only a note
Still quivers, goes out,
Revives, quivers, goes out.
From the sea no voice is heard:
Now we hear on all boughs

[15]

The clattering
Of silvery shower
That cleanses,
The clattering that varies
According to the bough
More thick, less thick.
Listen!
The daughter of air
Is silent; but the daughter
Of the mire, far off,
The frog
Sings in the midst of shadow
Who knows where, who knows?
And it rains on your eyebrows,
Hermione!

It rains on your black eyebrows
So that you seem to be crying,
But from pleasure; not white
But turned almost verdant,
You seem to come out of bark.
And the whole life is fresh in us,
Odorous,
The heart in our breast is like
A peach untouched.
Between the lids our eyes
Are like springs amid herbs,
The teeth in their sockets
Like bitter almonds.
And we go from bush to bush
Now joined now loose
(And the green rough vigor
Binds our ankles,
Entangles our knees),
Who knows where, who knows!
And it rains on our
Sylvan faces,
It rains on our
Gloveless hands,
On our light
Clothing
On the fresh thoughts

That the renewed soul
Discloses,
On the beautiful fable
That yesterday
Beguiled me, today beguiles you,
O Hermione!

Gabriele D'Annunzio
(1864-1940)

THE COMB

(*Villa Medici from Belvedere*)

Since on Monte Mario the sun-fires are extinguished,
The clouds come in slow swarms from the Palatine.

Mildly the wind's puff gathers them and drives them to the ocean
Where the cypresses pierce them with their sharp tops.

Then the black cypress tops are bitten by the clouds
Which flow as golden hair flows in a long comb.

Gabriele D'Annunzio

SUSPIRIA DE PROFUNDIS

Who to my pillow finally can lead
Sleep once again? Who gives me a little rest?
You, O dear hands, you that, when I am with death,
Will close my eyes deprived of any light
(I will not see that final gesture, God).
Can't you do so that I may fall asleep?

Oh, sweet thing in the night to be asleep!
Oh, sweet thing on an easy bed to sleep!
What have I done, what have I done, my God?
Why do you now deny to me this rest
I'm asking for? You see, I renounce the light.
May I be blind! I yield, you see, to death.

She well may come and take me—icy death—
Into her arms. I yield. To be asleep
In those her arms, and never to see light,
To close for ever the dry eyes to sleep!
Ah, for what reason, then, do you deny
This rest to me? What have I done, O God?

Gabriele D'Annunzio

THE WHITE ROSE

The white rose he gave you that day—how his
Big hand was trembling—do you still remember?
Yours, too, was trembling. And he said to you:
"It is the nicest growing in my garden."
Spotless the flower between you shone like
A taper in a church, and all was silent.
White roses, now that it's May, white roses in
Your garden shine immaculate; but you
Do not pick them; no one now picks out
The nicest rose for you; and from another
Hand you will have another rose no more.

Ada Negri
(1870-1945)

NOTHING I AM, O LORD

Nothing I am, O Lord,
On earth, and nothing is this earth
In the universe. And really I don't know
Where I come from, nor where I am going; deep, deep darkness
Before Your Will called me down here; blind hope
In your clemency, beyond the ultimate goal.
Unique reality: this is my nothingness,
Love moving on a narrow bridge suspended
Between two banks unknown to any of us:
And underneath an ever-flowing river
Noisily surges, and in the sky above
Burn incomprehensible the words of stars.
What do You want of me? What kind of present
Do You ask of my misery, and with what light
Will You amaze my soul on the blessed day
When she revives in You? But never You
Unveil Yourself. And it's in Your hidden thought
That I most search and pray: it's in this anguish
To know from You what You conceal from me,
That I draw strength to love You, O my Lord—
And great is my torment, great as is your silence.

Ada Negri

PAINFUL MEETING

Trembling with anxious hope,
My hand,
Lightly touches yours.
Touching it feels
A little golden ring:
Which seems to be burning,
Yet it is cold.
The fingers
Swiftly withdraw,
Painfully
In the speechless goodby.
A bitter smile
Of convenience
Furrows my face
Which feigns to meet
An old acquaintance.

Bruno Agazzi

DRY BUSH

I would like to have the cheerful soul
Of an ancient shepherd!
He drove the woolly animals
With a long rod; and he invoked his God,
Sure of his beliefs.
He traveled over boundless plains,
Jocund valleys,
And fallow-lands . . . And heard the beasts
Rattle beside ravines, on stony shores,
Among the arid bushes, full of thorns . . .

Like a dry bush is this border
Of the extreme reason
That wants to acknowledge the profiles
Of each faith, each anxiety, and each end . . .
Oh, if I had instead, simple and sure, the heart
Of an ancient man, happy
Leader of flocks!
A plenteous heart
Shining like a bush in April!

Claudio Allori

WITH A SHUDDER

With a shudder you shook your head,
And your vaporous hair
Wrapped you graciously.
My dream was pressing you:
My flesh
Was crying for love
As if it were wild . . .
A kiss
I caught in the air,
And I took
A sip of happiness . . .
But your eyes
Reflected
A heart of ice.

Augusto Arrigoni

THE INVISIBLE CADENCES

It seems joy to us,
The blooming of beardless skin,
The voice that leaves
The infantile tones,
The foot that lengthens
To put on men's shoes.

We would like to retain them
In an echoless expectancy . . .

But everything you bring, O Time,
Is riches to death,
Resounding while the years elapse
Like a sedate water-clock
Which beats in your blood
Invisible cadences.

Michelangelo Mazzeo Barmich

AND MY VOICE WAS CLOSED BY HERS

The flight of birds is bending
In the growing dusk of the evening
Panting with trees and tremblings.
The air covered with clouds,
On high toward the moon,

Which thinly appears through them
Smelling of the silence of the wood.

And I am still walking,
Near the tree
Which saw me happy and dreaming.
There I stop my cautious steps
And prick up my ears.

Perhaps tonight she is coming late;
She has to place
The ewe-lamb with her mother,
She must milk the last cow,
She has to refresh her face
And her soft hands.

She is coming already on the path:
Her steps make a noise
Of scattered leaves.
Some bough, meeting with her hair,
Trembles;
She removes it gently
And advances, thoughtful and attentive.

Her face radiates
Through the openings in the leaves.
   "My darling, anxiously
   I was waiting for you!"
And my voice was closed by hers.

Michelangelo Mazzeo Barmich

TO MY MOTHER

In the sad hour when I am feeling stronger,
O Mother, the nostalgia of your smile,
Of a caress, of a soft tender sigh,
Sweet is to me to recollect the past
And still I listen, as in sweet enchantment,
To your beloved voice and soft whisper.

And when in the anguish of the evening dusk,
In anxiety and torment, in the silence
That overwhelms my heart, you are far from me,
Very near to me I feel your pious figure,

And consolation offered by your eyes,
A consolation only you can impart.

And when a sweetness inundates my heart
And within me, whose age is that of dreams,
Is echoing the harmony of the universe,
And a hundred golden tresses and blue eyes,
Oh, then, too, in my breast the heart exults,
And nearer to you, Mother dear, I feel.

When I by night look sadly at the sky
And notice the refulgence of the stars,
Inside my soul there shines a brighter light
Encompassing the image of the heart,
And as a balm your ardent mouth lays down,
Slowly, a kiss upon my weary brow.

Francesco Berloco

INNOCENT SMALL BILLS*

There is a distant chirping of nestlings
Now that April dissipates the clouds
With the mild sun,
And the brier dresses up
For silent festivals.
A low chirping of innocent small bills,
A rustling lost in the sobbing of winds
On tender leaves
Like a fragile veil
On the apple tree's bough.

There is also a whimpering of children in the world,
Far from the heart. Yet they are children
Of man, and in their cry
There is a frightened call for mamma;
And they are motherless.
The wind on the apple tree and brier, mildly sings
Again its lullaby to the small nests:
But the orphan thinks,
Weeping, of his mamma,
Who . . . with a ghastly voice
Shows him a Cross.

Carlo Bianco

————

*Awarded a Bronze Medal at the great contest of
Brenta, for monument to Emilio Salgari—1950, Venice.

WINTER IMPRESSIONS

A veil of dream and mourning
Upon the motionless,
Languid, monotonous earth.

Arms of sharpened forms
Which cut the wind—
Remaining still—in vain
Stretched toward the sky,
Silent to our prayer.

Vision that, moved to pity, from a window
Shaped like a cross, perches
Upon the coping's smoke, light
As a fume of weeping
Or perhaps breathing the soul of people
That grieve and warm themselves.

Within the cypresses, thick with memories
Along the road to the place of death,
Alight the sad thoughts
Of my soul,
And an obscure anguish of silences,
Moist with tears,
Lays on the pallid face of the world
A gelid hand upon the heart.

Alvaro Bongi

NOT TO DIE

Still a small boy, I envied the hard sculptor
Who, cutting with the purest blades
The steadiest marble,
Was raising tombs in which
Corpses became corrupt, yet lived
In memory, and reached
In a halo of beauty and mystery
The farthest ages. Not real monuments
Of death, but challenges
Against death. And today, death and oblivion
Are always, anyhow, the enemies of
My stubborn heart; and pleasing
It is to ask myself if perhaps even these
Buildings of aerial words

[23]

Upon light sheets are not like them,
After their manner, compact shining blocks
Of marble, chiseled by my tenacious will
In spotless plates,
That last as long as perfect sepulchers.
Though only one of them outlive the rest,
It will retain that name which is more mine
Than my own bones. To dust,
Little by little will be reduced—together
With its sardonic laugh—my skull,
From calcined color; but a name, impalpable
In the impalpable kingdom
Of minds, will be
The Vanquisher of worms and Gods.

Aldo Capasso

SWALLOWS

The sky is very clear;
It is like the beautiful face
Of a smiling child.
The swallows are passing, flying;
They are arrows cutting the blue air;
They are small crosses vibrating
With lively whispers, shrieks,
And cries.
They keep in their rosy bills
Meadowy tender grass,
Twigs of blooming peach tree,
Violets, songs,
And, while every flower awakes,
They interweave around the windows
Delightful garlands of love.

Antonio Cappa

POET'S LAMENTATION

Her saddened hair, all ruffled,
Avidly kissed by the wind,
Beat on my face,
While sitting on the debris.
Villa Ermea!
How many dreams
And how many caresses!
But one day it happened

That the hair flew away,
Swept by the wind,
Ravished.
I go; I curse the wind.
I hate and adore it.
By night I like to rove
Among the widespread mist
While things are moaning:
Lightnings, thunderbolts,
The shuddering roar
Of thunder and blasts.
In the supreme empyrean!
Oh, that God, nature,
Had not given me
The most severe and horrid punishment:
An eager soul and open intellect!

Rolando Certa

WAR

Claws
In throat.

Throbs
Of bloody
Bleatings.

And darkness . . .

Madness
Excavating
A common
Grave.

Roberto Cervo

VICTORY

Voiceless
Laurels
Laid
Upon horrified
Marbles.

Cypresses
Shedding
Blood
At the roots.

Roberto Cervo

DO NOT AWAKE MY DREAMS

Do not awake my dreams,
Do not lay bare
My heart to the world's tragic sneer.

Peace, I invoke you always,
To the bitter vigils
Of my long indefatigable days,
Vain to my longings, to the hopes
That sink into my veins alluringly.

And I dream in the sunlight
As one does by night.

I dream, afar from human squabbles,
From dubious hates and shabby competitions.

Awake me never,
O men who rush to wrath, to blood:
I never will belong to you!

Roberto Cervo

WITHOUT A LANDING

Feather of sky, O lonely moon who lingers.
Intrusting idle stories to the wind,
Oh, I don't know how many times till now
I followed you in an eternal shipwreck.
And always on my forehead, softly you
Spread your caress of fairy while I was
Enchanted at the echoes of the night
By the stars, glittering in the space immense.
Slowly you passed, in candor, very high
Among the numerous reefs of clouds that seemed
Scared in the boundless ocean of deep silence.
The slumbering plain beneath was offering you
Its branchy arms from the belabored furrows,
And you, solemnly, O moon, were going on
Without a goal, toward the gloomy horizon,
Without a landing that might give you rest.

Roberto Cervo

ENIGMA

To Aldo Capasso

How long we cried embittered to the wind,
The wrath of ghosts turned pale at the faint sun
In the huge void that knows not what to tell us.
We never, to be sure, will hear all veins
Beating together at the dazzling lights,
The music of sighs full of tenderness.
Our simple hearts are raving as we see
The mud that plopped from distant mountain tops
Laughing and scoffing at the useless rubbish,
And from the booming street so full of crowds.
Ai, never reaches us an echo of peace
Devoid of cheat or filthy imposture. Only
Glum skies are covering themselves with dark,
Goading at our hallucinated eyes
Rabid and very greedy birds of prey.

Roberto Cervo

CLIMBING THE SKY

High, there above, is the azure canopy
Where flowers shine (and they are real worlds),
And shadows wander in disquieting tempos.
Mysterious is the voice inviting me
To ascend. A ladder that never ends.
It's rough and anxious. And in vain I look for
My sky (how far!) and I have lost the earth,
Alone, without an echo, is my voice
In the deep silence of the cosmic night.

Luigi Fiorentino

YOUNG GIRL

Gaily you are running in the fields,
And the air seems to enjoy it,
Young girl.
And all is green, is blue: it belongs to you.
Everything from you revives: it pants
Of the light wave that rounds your breasts:
Young girl, spring.

Creature of rose; looking at you
I feel I am made of soul, and at a nod of yours
I rise to a mountain summit,
And joy to me is your dream of eternity.

Unknowing! You fear nothing.
                              And such beauty
Is going to sink at the lost season's darkness,
And snow will fall upon your ambered hair:
The peach of face undone . . .
Young girl, O made of air, O light!
To stop spring,
The candid charger of your candid dreams,
And in the sea profound of these eyes
To have forever the image of you,
Gaily running in the fields,
And the air seeming to enjoy it,
Young girl!

                              Luigi Fiorentino

I WAIT FOR A TWILIGHT

This is the home. Here within these walls
We were happy, at times. The walls still
Exist, I touch them.
But where are gone *those* days?

In them we felt immersed
Like fruit swollen with juices
At golden noons.
The days were skimming this stone
As if on tiptoe, not to disturb us;
As, passing by, my fingers now
Touch it stealthily.

They turned the corner, never to come back.
They vanished with the vapors of twilight.
Where now are those days?
Now, on the roadway, look, a new twilight
Descends. Ah, always this arriving
Of twilight! Always, ah, this fraudulent
Stealing the days from us!

Among shadows I am still here: survivor
Of the days, as temporary
Derelict, striving against the swollen river.
But I am waiting for a twilight which,

At the unbounded mouth of days now lost,
Me too, and forever,
Me too, me too, will overthrow.

Lionello Fiumi

I HAVE TAKEN LIVES

Don't say I'm good. I, too, have taken lives.
Yet they didn't ask for anything except
A humble living, even with the ground,
Nor did they bear the haughty man ill-will.
Are they not satisfied
With any seed, with a small blade of grass?
They feasted when they had a drop of dew,
Paradise was for this one a sunray,
For that one, even darkness.

I killed them. Not in open war; not even
The sharp voluptuousness of risk!
With empty indifference,
As if one would pull off a leaf and just
A minute later think no more of it.

You see, I think of you because I want to, O victim
Of a moment ago, infinitesimal
Corpuscle. You had fallen on a sheet
And with your wonderful, so little paws
You were running, ignoring . . .

Sublime heroism of poet
Whose verses fashion beauty!
A crime: oh, yes! Or do I think, perhaps
To be, because your body is small, absolved?
A murderer is measured by the yard?
They, too, are creatures: in the boundless compass
Of the universe.
They, too, lives' dust; and in those iridescent
Winglets, in those small eyes, which like
Our eyes perceive,
And in that motion of contrivances,
Invisible yet perfect, don't you feel,
You, proud man, the reflection of the Almighty?

O Sovereign, I accuse myself. I killed
Creatures of Yours. I am not good: I killed.

Condemn me now to ponder on the patience
Of spiders, of the toiling, busy ants,
Of millepedes, as odd as ears of corn,
And on the gemmy pallet
Of certain caterpillars which I crushed
With ireful foot. How sweet it was, instead,
To take again to the open window
A rash maybug, and to see it
Vibrate, a golden humming in the sun!
Condemn me to remorse for all the beings
I have deprived of life!

And if I am about to cut away
A being, stop, I pray You, Lord, this hand!

Lionello Fiumi

ABSENCE

O mother, last night I had
A bitter illusion:
It was a torment.
I was burning, perspiring,
And piercing the dark with my eyes,
I was always looking for you.
A burning heat,
An anxious sigh; nobody around me.
Then my voice became faint,
My head was thundering:
I was dying!
O mother, if you are absent from my side,
I die for you!

Pino Giacopelli

NOCTURNE

I delude myself listening to distant sounds,
Looking in the void for the strange mystery
By which we are deprived of peace.
In the immovable opalescence of my thoughts
I turn my eyes fascinated
To the immense starry cavalcade
To seek in the unknown universe

For the reflection of your glance,
The echo of your words
Which are vanishing
In the limitless clear night,
And to live then in a dream's ecstasy.
But the cruel silence writes
The only thing alive, the remembrance of time
Which in the silent night evades
Together with the glimmer of
A cigarette's embers.
My sad and lonely heart
Is like a large and bloomless oasis,
A bush beyond the hedge
Without a nightingale's nest.
I would like with my fancy's wings
To rise up in the mist of every evening
To soar above in search of a friendly star
That sings to me above youthful love!

Eugenio Gnecchi

OLD TIMEPIECE

O little heart who are beating in the night,
A living being among the speechless things:
Only a watch, well knowing my inward fight,
You hide the secret of my sufferings.

You're lulling me to sleep, and your song brings
Annoyance, smelling also of a slight
Dejection. Maybe of this my life that stings
You shorten the few hours that still are bright

And lengthen those of my cruel destiny.
You, though alone, remain my faithful friend . . .
And tell me many things I long to hear.

You speak of love, of happiness and glee,
Of a bright flower plucked by a rough hand,
Of life that fades and Death who is drawing near.

Antonio Manuppelli

[31]

FOG UNDER THE MOON

The silver roofs
Are covers of biers
For the living asleep.
The houses, of white sugar—
Under the opaline clearness—
Are lying squat around,
Scared to look at
The black clot of wood.
Beneath the vault of the sky,
Sketched in light-dark,
The mountains watch
Over the dying day.
A shadow slips
Out of a door,
Beats the paving-stones
And hurls up to the stars
A short sob—
A worry
As great as the world.

Antonio Manuppelli

SPRING

Who knows why
These withered leaves of March
That shriek, whirling,
Through the clean swept streets
Or the lone alleys in the suburbs,
Are not like those snatched away
By the sad autumn,
But conceal in their melancholic farewell
Something
That recalls to our mind the slender girl
Who pines away and dies—
When life is rising again!
In Spring.
On the streets
Halved by the shadows of houses
Under a dazzling sun,
The wind drags in the mud
The last feeble echo of storm,
Which the night

Hid in the shrine of shadow.
Then the sun protects itself
Among fringes of woolly clouds,
Like the round face of a little girl
In the red frame of a window
Surrounded by hawthorn.
On the grey terrace,
There above,
A fair-haired little head,
Sad from overdreaming,
Asks the wind to bring
To the gentleman who is far away . . .
A short exhortation, a whisper:
"Come back!"

Antonio Manuppelli

ADOLESCENCE

Kiss me on the forehead,
My sweetheart,
As one kisses
The forehead of a child.
Although I am so old
That a child cannot be,
My heart is still as it was
In my childhood:
Pure and innocent,
A small heart
Of an adolescent.

Kiss me on the forehead,
O sweetheart:
Tonight
I am in pressing need
Of caresses.

Salvatore Maturanzo

[33]

CHRISTMAS—YOUNG SHEPHERD

The young shepherd
Walks behind the flock
Which, jingling,
Slowly ascends the mountain
And looks for grass.
He wears a broad-brimmed hat,
A large coat
Of velvet,
With grey and golden buttons.
Whistling,
With his rod
Now this, now that sheep,
Little by little,
Driving onward,
Slowly
The young shepherd
Ascends the mountain . . .
And looks tired.

Carmine Manzi

THE TRUE LIGHT

Every flower,
When spring passes away,
Loses its fine perfume
And lacks color . . .
But you, flower of every season,
The more you grow beautiful, the sweeter you smell.

After the clear day
Follows the dark night,
For, the sun having set,
Even the blue sky darkens . . .
But you are a pure source,
You always shine by your open light.

You are the star
Which never goes out at dawn,
You are the rose
Which does not lose its leaves,
You are my true light,
You are the eternal Spring.

Carmine Manzi

MAN SPEAKS

I first used to look at the immense
Expanse of the sea,
The blooming hills and the blue
Of the clear sky;
I used to look dreaming at the beach
On which silently broke
The placid foam,
The vine-tendrils at the wind
Of the soft lethargic April.
But now I do not dream,
I do not plunge my body any more
In the water of the clear brook,
But I look at the heavy rain
Showering from the sky,
I lay hold of the plough and till
The fruitful earth,
I tear its bosom and plant
The shrub which fears no wind,
I plant the oak that defies
The storms of the sky:
O tenacious strength of muscles!
O life! I am the man who speaks,
Who wants to forge his destiny
Only with Labor!

Guido Massarelli

THE RUNAWAY

Soiled with mud and dust, his hands all stained with blood,
Cadaverous, confused, livid, he appeared on a sudden before me.

"Shalom!" he shouted. "Brother," I said, "where do you come
    from?
Who ruined you like that? who inflicted those wounds on you?"

"I ran away from Rome, I flew from the new cruel Egypt,
As the ancient fathers flew from the ancient one.

"Like them I walked bent under the yoke of heavy blocks,
And very heavy stones pressed my aching nape.

"From dawn to evening bowed down like a laboring ox,
But not at all resigned, not subdued nor overcome.

"I carried mortar and rocks of anguish in the burning sun,
Under the water that macerates stones of tedium and sand.

"But soaked with water and sunburnt, I thought of escape
Which redeems the oppressed, sets free the chained.

"And lo, I stole away from the hard ties of the great City
Which is cementing its walls with our blood and tears.

"With a small bundle of worthless rags I ran away,
Bowed by a grim load of anguish and bitter weeping:

"All the anguish and the weeping of our brothers who moan
Under the scourge, amazed at being enslaved again.

"They look with dimmed eyes at the horror of the day that is gone,
With glassy eyes they look at the horror of daybreak.

"Oh, new Egypt, oh, Red Sea of blood without a passage
To Sinai that may shine from deserts up to the sky!"

The runaway weeps, I weep, I welcome him with a brotherly kiss,
I bandage his wounds, I soothe and alleviate his pains.

I want him to stay at my home, to rest among the green,
So he may be consoled with olive trees and vine-tendrils.

Angiolo Orvieto

VENETIAN VISIONS
Reflections
In the light golden atmosphere
Of Venetian sunsets
Pass through the city of doges
Dazzling lights
In a gentle tremor—
And the *rios*, the canals,
Soft, velvety, mossy,
Are lighted with the strangest colors.

Laminae of fire,
Arrows of purple,
Flares of sapphire and amethyst,
Of chrysoprase and opal
On the gliding drowsy ways
Of august infinity,
Suspended in space and time.

And creep, dance, swing,
Vanish, reappear, turn about,
Pirouette serpentine,
Volutely, spirally
The reflections of architecture
Of bridges,
Of buildings and patrician marbles
Set with gems under water
In fantasies of dream . . .
In sidereal flowers,
In rainbows,
In jewels of constellations
On crystalline skies
And on mute-caressing and fearful—
Legends of deities and sirens.

An overturned,
Upside down, tottering, joking,
Flying, dancing city
Which, reflected, frolics
In plays of interlacements
And fancies of lights
With its palaces, belvederes,
Balconies, towers,
Gondolas, and with its sleepy arches.

A poem level with water
Of a silent fabled world
Incomprehensible, unexpressible,
Wandering on the wavy metal
Of the drowsy canals
With the mystery of Venetian charm,
Which receives the breath of centuries . . .

A charm that, as the night descends,
Vanishes on a sudden
And at the buoy of the dark waves
In a whiteness of pearls
Is engulfed! . . .

Ennia Clarice Pedrocco

THAT SMOKE . . .

That smoke I would like to be,
Son of the ravenous flame
Which furiously frees itself
From the furnace,
And rising
Through scorched fireplaces
Up the chimney-pot,
Overflows to quench its thirst
In fresh liberty:

Just for the voluptuousness
To feel myself
Burn and extinguish,
Then dissolve in the enchantment
Of this clear windy evening.

Gino Rovida

SHORT ELEGY

A flower on every grave
In the garden of the dead.
Nostalgia of blood and lukewarmness
In the whitened hearts
Under the turned-up earth:
Yearnings, spasms,
In the dream of memories.

And you passed. With the light
Fluttering of dragon-fly,
Warm with manifold senses,
Queen of joy, you passed
Among the graves strewn with flowers:
On the wind your hair was waving
Like a mourning veil.

At the spreading of your ray
The crosses lighted up;
Underneath, in funereal grandeur,
The hearts felt your passage
And regretted the life they had lost:
While, O daughter of Eva,
Having grown austere and fleeting,
Your beauty was weeping.

Gino Rovida

ULYSSES

I navigated in my youth along
The rough Dalmatian coasts and shores. Islets
Emerged, level with water, on which seldom
A bird, intent on preying, stopped or paused,
Covered with sea-weeds, slippery in the sun,
As pretty as emeralds. When the high tide
And the night-shadows nullified them, sailors
Leeward were listing offshore, to avoid
The snare of hidden reefs. Today *his* kingdom
Is that land which belongs to none. The harbor
Turns on its lights for others. Me to the offing
Still pushes my indomitable spirit
And this my dolorous true love of life.

Umberto Saba

OH, MY MELANCHOLY!

The conversation with the evening starts.
The light of day is slowly vanishing;
    Darkness spreads over all.
I sit at an imaginary balcony
To penetrate the stars and the dark green
    Of the eternal cypresses.
Through arid paths, down yonder in the background,
No step resounds, except a twittering song
    Of a sad, lonely blackbird.
A covert peace descends upon the earth,
Noiseless and gentle, to transform all things
    In my mystic harmony.

Oh, my melancholy!
In bold vine-branches and in strange contortions
You come up from the balcony, expanding
    And wrapping up my soul.
You are not deceit, but a tormenting flame
Which comes from the heart and fecundates itself
    In it. You are my creature.

Anna Maria Stocchino

FARM HAND

He used to stop working
When the glowing
Sun's globe
Seemed to fall upon his back.
He was always a grumbler.
Like a faithful dog
He loved his master.

Geppo Tedeschi

MILLER'S APPRENTICE

They granted him rest
After sunset.
They woke him up in a hurry
At daybreak.
He always held his tongue.
His companions were
The green frog
And the mill cricket.

Geppo Tedeschi

LIZARD

A stone lizard,
On the edge
Of an old road
With twisted hedges,
Shows, reversed,
The grey of its abdomen,
Contemplation of olive-tree,
On life and death.

Geppo Tedeschi

NEW MOON IN MAY

It is very ingenuous,
This new moon.
Yesterday,
For a few fables of wind,
It gave to the cane-brake
Silver and silver.

Geppo Tedeschi

SELENE

Old uncontaminated queen,
You are so pale tonight.
The bad news comes perhaps to you
From here below
That men would like to own you?
I see already from your horrid clefts,
Dripping
Copious and red,
Fraternal blood.
Run away,
Do, so that the menace may vanish.
Immense you are
Because unknown.
Your mystery keeps us spell-bound.
Tomorrow it will be too late.
You will be contaminated,
Darkened:
You will stop being a star,
You will become Earth,
You will be lost.
Poets will forsake you,
And my lyre
Will sob.

Giuseppe Trucco

O MOUNTAIN, HAIL!

Hail,
O green hope of woods,
O immense shudder of pines,
O steadiness of rocks,
O thirst for the infinite!

Mingled with a thousand harmonies
Is the voice of streams,

A yearning,
The voice of the distant valley.

Summit carved in the sky,
Craving for the tops
Is torment,
The call to whirlwinds
Anguish,
The invitation to purity
Is passion.

Hail, Hail, O mountain!
On the granitic rocks
Which cut the air
Body and soul are in strife . . .
And the wave breaks and the rocks
Remain
Powerful and everlasting:
It is God who answers.

Sandro Venturini

HAPPINESS

O Happiness, within your shaded eyes
Shines the rejoicing of the morn immense;
You speak the motion of our life, the gay
And festive sense of things born from the night
With the sweet rhythm of every slender stalk,
With the festivity of sparrows on
The boughs, with dawn drawing embroideries
Of gold on the vast circle of the sky.
O Happiness, you are mine. Within your hands,
That know the sweet caress which lulls to sleep,
There is the soft, slow music of the air
When it is blowing 'mid the alder leaves.
Your hair is carrying with it the perfume
Of orange-flowers in May, and your fine mouth
Binds like the resin which is flowing from
The bark of the stone-pines in copious clots.
O Happiness you are mine. You're cloud and flower,
In the sky or on the earth, truth and idea,
You're soul and body, human form and goddess,
Far from my heart and in my very heart.

Giuseppe Villaroel

TENDERNESS OF YOU

Tenderness of you I feel, O pallid love,
When the moon slowly among the olive-trees rises
And makes, aslant the street, the water shiver
Amid the pines of country-seats, immobile.
The mountains are dissolving in the sky
In an inhuman silence. Alas, how
Survives the white enchanting nudity
Of all your forms in this vast solitude
Of the earth that is so sorrowful! My heart
Aches when I think that you are lost. And to me
Remains the wonder that I feel alive.

Giuseppe Villaroel

I AM TWENTY YEARS OLD

I am twenty years old.
No joy I know
Of the happy world I dreamed
When I was a child.
My heart has grown old
And its beat gets lost in time.
My youthful years remember only
Mournings and smoke of houses,
And booming of bombs, and the dead,
And wailing of folks
Beside a red-hot brick.
Wherever I turn my eyes
There is sadness of things: of men!
And my heart is pinched by grief . . .

I am twenty years old.
I love the mere life that forged me
And the world where I was born,
The great things of the new man,
But I have no father and: I have just brothers
Who fight, and friends and comrades: everywhere.

I am twenty years old.
And we are millions of working men
Who do not know frontiers . . .
We are millions of workers in a group
Whom time has forged to the idea:
Who struggle,
And love the great things of the new man.

Dante Volpintesta

[43]

FALERNIAN AND LETHE

The butterfly from a flower
Is sucking pollen . . .
I pass by without looking at her:
My heart is very sad.
The green lizard vibrates
In the heat and enjoys herself on a stone.
Gloomily resounds my step:
Because I have lost my love.
A friend invites me
To a fraternal symposium.
But where is my life?
My thirst will be quenched
Not by the old Falernian wine,
But by the dark Lethean waters.

Carlo Weidlich

SWEETNESS

A rivulet of sweetness
Is flowing into my heart
And slowly inebriates me,
Perfume of resin in thick forests.
Thus I go toward my goal,
Whence sound eternity's tones.
O sweetness, now that you are mine
And I enjoy you voluptuously,
Try to remain for ever
At my dinner-table,
Companion to a poor poet.
If you leave me, sweetness,
Who will give me the last smile?

Armando Zamboni

THE ONE I WAIT FOR

In the silence of starless night
I hear a plushy step approaching.
It is close by, and my heart startles;
But lo, the step sounds already far.

Thus will come the one I wait for,
And would not dare to invite:
From unknown regions
She will come stepping softly
Until she reaches my ankle-bones.
I will, then, not rebel,
As, having left my bag,
Taken off my heavy shoes,
With her, pitiless, I will proceed lightly
Beyond the threshold of mystery.
Armando Zamboni

II

ITALO-AMERICAN POETS

Translations by Rodolfo Pucelli

TO MY YOUTH

O doleful youth that were so full of pride
Once, and so bold none could on you impose,
You lasted only like a charming rose
Which lasts from sunrise to the coming night.

They knocked you down with all their wicked might,
O youth of mine that were so bellicose!
Now you are dead who once without repose
Disdainfully the storm of life defied.

Now you have nothing left but my complaint,
As all the women who loved you once so much
Turn, passing by, from you their sneering eyes.

Now you have nothing left but my lament
And suffering, as the world that is—fie—such
A cruel cheat, says scoffingly! "He dies!"

Riccardo Cordiferro

POETRY

When in my heart resounds the tone
Of poetry, so dear and sweet,
I'm like a beggar to whom someone
Offered a necklace in the street.

I'm like a sleeper in a garden
Who wakes up at the fall of white
Petals that whisper, dance, and wander
Lightly before they, tired, alight.

I'm like a prisoner full of grief
To whom one a love-letter hands.
The jail is no more dismal, if
With harmony my heart expands.

Severina Magni

[49]

PARTING

The day was near to sundown.
Over the slender poplar top
A flight of cheerful swallows.
The valley slept in the shadow,
A song of women, a sob
Drifted from the old fountain . . .
In our souls a sudden startle.

A group of golden clouds
Wandered above the bluish mountains;
The crickets chirped in the meadows.
In the sky the horned moon
Shone amid glittering stars;
In the calm air, tollings
Of near and distant bells.

A fragrance of vermillion roses
Came from the rosebush near;
A rumble of trains afar
Shook us with lugubrious howl.
We shuddered. Saying farewell,
Three times I kissed her hand,
Three times I pressed her to my heart!

Florio Vitullo

PEASANTS

O tired enduring folks who live to break
The hard ground with the smooth and shining plough,
Your parched foreheads in perspiration bathed
Under the kiss of the beloved sun,
While the swallow returns to her old nest
She left to migrate to some warmer clime.

Unknown, forgotten soldiers of the soil,
Heroes of spade and shovel, O ye strong
Offspring of ancient ancestry, whose hearts
Are utterly devoid of useless glories,
The good white bread you give to the whole world,
And you are feeling oft the want of it.

You are so poor, and yet serene and healthy;
You spade the bare and arid ground of farms,
While the tree slowly adorns itself with buds
And in the light the sky grows blue again,
And every humble flower raises its head
To greet you always, O good-hearted folks.

Upon your backs, bent over to perform
Your holy work, descend the hot sun's rays,
But satisfied and conscious of your strength
You mow down in the field the ripening ears,
Giving your boss, or master florid crops
Which from the fertile soil your toil has won.

Sons of the farm, the sun is smiling on you,
The quiet moon is blandly smiling, too,
While in the sky a choir of fulgent stars
Are singing in their language: "There is no
Happiness found in wealth for any man,
Happy alone the man who lives by work."

Florio Vitullo

PRAYER FOR PEACE

God of the sky and the whole universe,
O Supreme wisdom, intellect, and love,
O law eternal ruling over truth,
Father of man and maker of all things,
We turn our thoughts to You, for You alone
Are well acquainted with our inward wish,
God of the sky and the whole universe.

We pray You, help us, ere it is too late!
We feel exhausted, grieved, and desolate.
The fault is in our stubborn cowardice.
Hatred we have, because we are ungrateful;
We have been false and liars, bad in our work.
We pray You, help us, ere it is too late!

Answer, O Lord, to our imploring voice,
As You alone can give us brain and help.
Humanity is chained and on the cross;
We all want peace, we eagerly want life,

[51]

Not total ruin, not a cruel war—
For our goodness and your endless glory.

We wish for peace and also bread and work.
The holy peace that makes us brethren all;
The peace which is a treasure of the soul,
Which makes faith strong and hope more beautiful;
And justice offers to it verdant laurels
With gracefulness and joy and gentle words.

John J. Alifano

LOVE AS RESCUER
To my dear Wife Helen

I was quite lost, and rescue was not near
(By whom was I then led, I'd like to know,
On a rough thorny way? by friend or foe?)
My whole life was reduced, ah! to a zero,
To a mere cypher that is called Chimera.

I don't know how I met you on that day.
O beautiful girl, O sunshine of my soul;
Yet from that happy day to a new goal
My life is going on a smoother way.
I don't know how I met you on that day.

This is the sunny way leading to glory,
Because I have been guided from the start
By your love which illuminates my heart,
I shall win in every field—no idle story!
This is the sunny way leading to glory.

You are my help and prop, and that sheer light
Of hope which beautifies our life—you are,
O sweetheart, that refulgent heavenly star
That leads me to the sphere so lofty and bright.
You are my help and prop, and that sheer light.

Oh, lead me, my sole leader, on forever,
Because, my Helen, in your hands did God
Place the tomorrow's secret, which for both
Of us is the true Word, failing us never.
Oh, lead me, my sole leader, on forever.

John J. Alifano

SPRINGTIME SONNET

You see, the earth is in festivity:
She donned her dress of velvet; everything
Created, not the sky alone and sea,
Invites a song on harps and lutes to sing.

And the sweet songs of smiles and harmony,
Of joy and peace and love did not yet bring
Relief to your profound melancholy,
O gloomy girl, who feel your suffering's sting!

Why don't you want to join in such a feast
Where Dian, Hygeia, Apollo, and Orpheus meet,
As well as Cupid and the Muses all?

Cheer up, my girl, and dissipate all mist.
Come on! my love will make your heart soon beat
With happiness: you're welcome to my soul.

John J. Alifano

MAN

Man: a superb and noble figure, is
Unknown even to himself. He is a thoughtful
And overbearing genius in his nature,
Who is born to die without enjoying rest:
Compound of boldness, hatred, and imposture,
Of love and indolence and pitiful pain.
Who ne'er will know in his long road wherefrom
He comes and whither he is going again.

Efrem Bartoletti

HYMEN'S KNOT

*On the occasion of the marriage of my niece Flora
and the young man Steve E. Rambert, Jr.*

In this great country, where
A starry flag is hoisted as a symbol
Of harmony, the various
Offspring of the whole world come up together.

Out of the combinations
So well assorted of prolific hymen,
New families are rising,
New families of real Americans.

[53]

And also Steve and Flora,
Hit in their youthful breasts by Cupid's arrow,
The indissoluble knot
Of hymen consecrated on the altar,

Seeing come true the beautiful
Dream of a love that was so deeply rooted
In the sweet hearts of two
Young persons born and raised in the same land;

Who have indeed in common
High aspirations, language, education,
And noble feelings toward
Their fatherland, in whose defense young Steve,

As airman-bombardier,
Speedily flying over borders, fought
Beyond the ocean, daringly,
Getting promotions and high honors too.

Oh, yes, also his father
And Flora's both enlisted volunteers,
Joined the American Army of their time
That went to Europe in the first World War.

Thus in the times gone by
Garibaldi, Kosciusko and the rest,
Unconquerable, fought for us,
The freedom of America and the world.

Examples all of altruistic thought,
Of solidarity and compactness
Among the various progeny
That of our nation form the unity.

Therefore from happy marriages
Of passionate love like that of Steve and Flora
Are rising by and by
New families of pure Americans.

Plinio Bulleri

THE NURSES

To the Nurses—Ward E 4—Veterans Administration
Hospital, Hines, Illinois

In the wards and rooms
Of the hospital
Stands forth the neatness
Of the candid gowns
Which, worn by the nurses,
Are fluttering white
As white wings of butterflies.

A going and coming of attendants
And experienced nurses
Devoted always
To assuage the sufferings
Of the sick entrusted
To their assiduous care.

Where assistance is most needed
By turn is watching
One of them,
Running up at the first moan
That with anxious breathing
The patient gives
From his chest;
And by the beat of his pulse
She intuits
The beat of the heart.

He fails to see her coming
But it seems to him he sees
With closed eyes
(As the strange and confused
Vision of a dream)
A faint gleam diffused
In the whole room.

He opens his eyes and the enchantment
Of the confused vision
Takes real shape
And sweetly smiles at him,
As when he was, sometimes,
A sickly child

And his mother smiled at him,
Dressed in a white bed-gown,
Watching the whole night through,
From evening to dawn,
At his bedside.

The heavy eyelids
Again he closes,
And the strange whiteness
Of the candid gown
Gets confused
With the neatness
Of that white bed-gown
Which insistently projects
Into his lifeless eyes
The vision
Of his distant infancy.

Plinio Bulleri

RITA AND JUDY

My grand-daughters, Rita and Judy,
Although very little—
They are both only five or six years old—
Have so many toys
That they could fill the show-windows
Of an archeologist
And an engineer's shop.

Roller skates,
Racing bicycles,
Automobiles and baby carriages,
And wooden horses on wheels;
Rifles and revolvers
To play at war and banditry.

Thus laden with arms,
To buy sweetmeats and ice cream,
They rob the banks
Of their small heaped up savings.

They arrange in good order
Elephants, camels,
Toy soldiers and quacks,
Rope-dancers and buffoons
Under white circus pavilions.

Pitched tents
For entire regiments
Of soldiers encamped in the open,
Disposed to set out
Accompanied by music
Of whistles, hand-organs, and pianos.

An intonation of deafening sounds
And songs
Louder and truer
Than gramophone records
And invisible programs
On the radio.

On a sudden they forego
All the other playthings
Attracted by the visible,
Horrifying and amusing television scenes,
Absorbed
In amazed contemplation.

Plinio Bulleri

CRY TO THE DESERT

Jesus one day was sitting on the steps
Of Israel's temple, and from there He taught
The ignorant crowd the meaning of God's law,
  When a large group of people who had got
Excited at a woman near undressed
And tired, who was ashamed and feared a lot,
  Came to Him, and a scholar, rather pressed
Elbowed his way and most inquisitive
Thus spoke to Christ, who listened unimpressed:
  "Master, that woman who seems full of grief,
Shame-faced, is an adulteress, you know,
Caught in the very act. No right to live,
  I think, has she. Moses, to whom we bow,

Gave us a holy law, by strength of which
She shall be lapidated. Tell us now,
   You who Jehovah extol, what shall we do
With this low wretch? She realizes well
Her guilt, and shudders at your lofty speech."
   Jesus, who was good-hearted and so wise,
Perceived the snare, and, disconcerted, down
He slowly bent His sweet and humble eyes,
   And with a finger, then, the still unknown
Fate He began to write upon the floor,
So that the answer to the man be known.
   But the rash people, who by an uproar
Mitres and crowns sometimes pull down, and yet
Justice and truth too often may abhor,
   Rose in behalf of that buffoon, so that
He might be approved. And Christ disdainfully
Looked at the silly crowd and told them straight:
   "Brethren, who happens among you to be
Sinless, may first against her throw a stone!"
And then, distressed, to write continued He.
   Both Scribes and Pharisees remained anon
Perplexed at such right words, and realized
They failed in scheming and their wits were gone.
   When suddenly one who was recognized
As the most dastard fellow by those wretched
Who formed the crowd by many so idolized,
   Picked up a stone, and stepping forth he stretched
His arm and beating her repeatedly
He cried: "Down with the harlot!" The other fetched
   More heavy stones and threw them angrily
Against the adulteress, until she fell
Down to the ground, and never rise could she.
   For such a justice, worthy of deep hell,
Jesus shed tears, and humble still and kind
Sits on the steps, and wishing all men well
   He dreams of the sweet kingdom of mankind.
Nino Caradonna

THE TWO ROADS

Long weighed with thought, I came to my decision.
There are two roads: one easy, another rough.
The former seems to lead to fields elysian,
The latter, to some deep beneath a bluff.

On cobbled road I set out smiling, gruff
To harm and building dreams against derision.
My hands and feet are bleeding, but enough;
It does not force me to my plan's revision.

The more I walk inside the noisome den,
The more the jagged rocks rend and oppress;
Yet a glimpse of hope makes me forget my plight.

What Genius does inspire and guide me then?
I do not know. He cries: "Fear no distress!
Strive, persevere, and you will find the Light!"

Antonino Crivello

THE BURNT TRICOLORE

(Bay St. Louis, Mississippi)

To tell the truth, it happened never before
Such a mean fact: the Immaculate Society
Burnt on the square the Italian *tricolore,*
As if to make a show of some variety.

And note that all the members, none except,
Adored that flag and made it proudly fly
In their parades, saluting from the depth
Of hearts: "For you we gladly fight and die!"

The crowd was bawling venomously, and
By order it was soaked with oil, unfurled,
Then grasped with spite by some unworthy hand
—Poor Italy's flag!—and put to fire and burned.

Who did this outrage? Ah, the president
Of the Society: a silly man,
Vainglorious, tough, devoid of sentiment,
Somewhat deranged, it may be, in his brain.

The glorious flag of the United States
Triumphantly was hoisted on the spot
Where the Italian had been burnt to ashes,
And soon the sight of stars and stripes we got.

There are some nations full of fantasy,
And savage men of the dark continent
Who dance in rites of anthropophagy,
Yet worse is that Italian president.

Americans like you, as all men know,
Are foolish, O low man, I feel ashamed.
You should be punished by American law,
Brought to the gallows—and by God be damned!

And you, O members of the Immaculate
Conception, are misled. You do not love
Your native country, nor this one, I state,
As you despised your Church and God above.

The incendiaries failed to understand,
Blinded with hatred as they were, that we
Are of America the faithful friends
And wish to live with her in amity.

How I would like to have a chance to see
The charming flags of our two noble nations
Flying together! We would be all free,
Nor be afraid of tyrants' desecrations.

Antonio J. Daraio

DAWN OF 1949
To My Wife Tina
After a score of years, with loyalty
I write for you of love, renew my vow,
With all the strength that God concedes to me
And with the blood that from my heart does flow.

I write for you while this my mind yields now
To the impulse of my heart, and fervidly
I thank Our Lord who to me here below
Gave once this flower filling me with glee.

As in the ancient times of myth I swear
That in this world there's nothing so divine
That may entice me or from you remove.

I live for you, for you who are so fair
(Oh, sacred dawn of nineteen-forty-nine!)
And I forget all worries in your love.

                                        Scipio Di Dario

HAIL!

To Liberato Trotta, Secretary of the *Associazione*
Ex Combattenti Felittesi, of Old Forge, Pennsylvania

From far, through mountains and a spacious plain,
I sing a hymn of love, and be it for
The affectionate, good-hearted countrymen
Of our own sunny *Valle del Calore.*

On this most happy day, united all
In a fraternal warm embrace, O bold
Arditi, the high feats you now recall . . .
A score of years elapsed . . . we are growing old.

And on the setting of a withered age
The soul unveils the cruel reality,
And points out calmly to the world the rage
Of war and all its frightful tragedy.

And dreams and disappointments, hopes; and still
The sad and bitter truth is not revealed . . .
We pray for days that never dawned on hill,
For things we cherish but are still concealed.

Already twenty years elapsed; the time
Of our bold youth returns to us no more;
And mothers full of grief in every clime,
Forsaken—ah! Almighty God implore!

And in the meeting of this happy hour
All smile at their inhuman destiny . . .
In this bright feast all seem to pick a flower
And sing the song of life and death with glee.

[61]

What do we sing, O gallant veterans?
The curse of Victory which, though so bright,
Gave us just tears and ruined all our plans,
Left us a world in fear by day and night.

To this, our mystic song, which fleeting is,
Bursts forth an echo from the grave obscure:
They are the heroes who have found their peace
In sleep, a home that always will endure.

And they, in this fraternal gathering
Will join, as twenty years and more ago,
To greet the veterans—and they will sing
To the deluded: "Love both friend and foe."

To the sweet hymn that crosses mount and plain,
Bringing the spell of love to every shore,
I want to add mine now: Hail, countrymen
Of the dear sunny *Valle del Calore!*

Scipio Di Dario

CLOUD

There is a cloud today in the sky
Astray in immensity . . .
It seems a fairy, in the short instant
Of a mystical voyage oversea . . .

You go your way, O baby of the sky,
Alone and happy . . .
Alone and happy . . .
Toward the infinite.
And the spring-sun accompanies you . . .
The supreme joy
Of being queen
Of a boundless horizon.

O light cloud,
My destiny is like yours.
I, too, am lost; but the road here below
Is rough and hard. At every step I stumble.
I'm not free to go . . .
As you are.

And wind and hurricane come along with me . . .
The dark night . . .
A sadness that befogs the heart.

O cloud of the sky,
With you I'd like to soar
In the vast blue
And follow your route
In a smile . . .
Up to paradise . . .

Perhaps, there above, in the magic splendor
Of stars and lights,
I would be able to find
The peace I have lost!

Giuseppe Di Gioia

RAIN

From the hilltop I'm looking down to the valley:
Mist descends
And cloaks the horizon
With a thick veil.
It is night.
The lightning flares
In a luminous disk
High in the sky.
Rain falls
Slowly, steadily:
It changes into sounding thuds
And reawakens the valley
With the harmony
Of children's voices.
And I, who am listening,
Immerse myself in jocund thoughts
Of other time: when, as a child,
I squeezed joy
From the muddy water.
Beautiful it is
To listen to the sky music
That recalls the past, in the depth of night,
When it is raining—
To melt into tears

The heart's sadness,
As the clouds in the sky
Melt into tears
Their sadness and pain.
Beautiful it is to retire
In an oasis of peace—
To forget—
And listen to a celestial chant,
The sound of a thousand voices
Departing from the sky!

Giuseppe Di Gioia

IF WE WOULD THINK . . .

If death were somewhat more within our mind—
Death that will surely come to us some day—
We would not be so tough, so unrefined
And rash; instead we would be good and pray.

An evil aptitude, a wish to stray,
Is in our body, thought, and soul enshrined,
And forces us to take the wrongful way—
To act as shamelessly as one long blind.

Instead of living in a brotherhood,
Bestowing mutual love, we lack restraint;
Hyena-like we each the other tear.

This is not real culture, or a good
And honest life . . . But vain is my complaint:
Man likes to live this way, and does not care.

Salvatore Di Leo

(Translated from Sicilian dialect)

AUTUMN IS COMING
I

Autumn is coming, and the leaves fall down,
The roses fade away upon their stalks:
So my hopes vanished, and I with a moan
Feel that my heart is cold and full of shocks.

Autumn is coming, and one hears no more
The twitter of the birds, before so gay;
They seem to weep, as if they had a sore,
For the past sunny days of heavenly May.

[64]

Autumn is coming, and the leaves fall down,
Just as the hopes of this my broken heart.

II

Autumn is coming, and my heart is full
Of grief and pines away in loneliness.
I think of her, who is so beautiful
And does not care, maybe, for my caress.

Autumn is coming, and I am sad and lone,
With my deep sighs and tears and inward pain.
I look in vain for her; my love is gone,
And I will never, ah, be happy again.

Autumn is coming, and I am sad and lone,
With my deep sighs and tears and inward pain.

Salvatore Di Leo

KHIM THE SAGE

Khim, who through deserts and savannas leads
The long and slowly advancing caravan
And wisdom draws from silence, while he reads
The eyes of Sphinx, a puzzle to any man,

Said: "On this earth there are, and were before,
Nine awful things, besides music and war:
Horses, and women, galleys, minarets
On top of mosques, the parching thirst that gets
A traveler, the impatience, if not rage,
Of him who waits, the experience of old age,
Vain, he who craves for justice to carry on,
And, finally, the vultures round a carrion.

Ali, whose leather bags and dromedaries
Laden with goods, is watching, says: "O Harry,
Why, to the list, our poets don't you add,
Who farther off than Death can see ahead
And higher than love, who mysteries can delve,
And who are honored by high Allah himself?"

Khim answered: "Ali, if I didn't do it, then
Remember that they are just nine, not ten."

Arturo Giovannitti

INVITING SPRING

I saw her this morning from my window sill.
She said to me: "Come out in the open, down!
I will give you a wreath of flowers grown
There in the valley bordering on the hill.

I wish you to listen to the brooklet's chant,
Blended with that of black-caps, and that you
May also feel the joys, those that are true
And fascinate, and make you even pant.

Come down! I've looked for you for many a day,
In vain. What has happened to you, dear?
Even the chirping birds—do you not hear?—
Upon the meadow, welcome you, all gay.

I have embroidered many a beautiful thing
And I am sure that they will do you good;
Only at sight of them you'll cease to brood
And be so happy that you smile and sing.

Come! do you see in the valley that peach tree?
What colors! and what fragrance comes from there!
I want a twig of it to put in my hair
Which will reach down my shoulders charmingly.

Today I want to look to you by far
More beautiful than ever in the years
Gone by, when you were praising me with cheers
As if I really were a morning star.

Oh, look at that magnolia! How dear!
It seems a group of sisters without scowls,
Who sing in chorus with their fervent souls
A sacred hymn that pleases those who hear."

Oh, if I could, O sister, as you can!
How many things I would like to renew!
But first I'd give all peoples, not a few,
The faith which will redeem, unite all men!

Francesco Greco

THE GODDESS ENVY

Among the toughest, vilest human figures
Who, like obscure and giant clouds,
Obstruct the earth
And kindle in peace-loving men
A furious, warlike spirit,
I am the most distressing.

Wherever I pass, on gloomy wing of death,
A blast of storm is going.
My eyes, perennially sleepless,
Indifferent to any pity
And which look dismally,
Insidiously on others' happiness,
Are green with spite and hatred.
A heap of viscid snakes
Has my corrupted heart.
My hair is disheveled
Upon my pale and wrinkled forehead;
I'm cold as snow;
I'm dressed with mud.
My titles are perfidiousness and rancor.
And my name is Envy!
When the moon shines in the blue sky
And everything is silent,
While the stars glare,
Divinely beautiful
In the depth of the night,
And men, forgetting all their ills,
Are taking rest,
I alone keep awake, and my malignant soul,
Like an ominous bird,
Hurls through the vast world asleep,
And unrestrained, all over
I pour abundantly
The fatal liquid of my poison.
An unrelenting torment seizes me
From head to foot and crushes my black heart,
If I see some elected spirit ascend
With shouts of joy and fieriness
To the sun's beaming ray and toward beauty.
I rejoice only when a vanquished creature
Precipitates into deepest emptiness;
When the wave of evil,
Like a menacing, turbid surge
Is rising to the stars;
When human beings
Are dirty and wretched,
And I alone majestically soar
Among a crowd of foolish, awkward people.

Pietro Greco

MENACE

Giant clouds
Pass across the livid sky
Menacingly.
A yellowish light
Is in the air, filtering
From a thin stratus
Of rust-colored fumes.
The face of the sky has lost
Its purest blue:
It has the pale hue
Of muddy soil.
It is the prelude of a storm.
Little by little, the wind
Unhinges the gates of the sky
And freely
Breaks into the air.
The powerlessness
Which kept it bound
With its iron law,
Has become a strength
That overcomes all obstacles.
The scared birds fly
From the trembling boughs;
The dogs run away;
In the air fly scraps of paper,
Torn leaves,
And blinding dust.
Through the farm and the cities,
Everywhere it passes,
Debauched devil,
It whistles, menaces, hurls down,
Uproots pitilessly.

Pietro Greco

THUNDER-STORM

Monsters of clouds,
With somber
And grim looks,
Rise from the north:

And the threatening wind,
Assembling them
Like a herd,
Hisses and whistles.

Whistles. The plants
Are bending
To the ground
Like bulrushes.

On high, a lightning flash
That blinds, creeps,
And quickly
Vanishes. It thunders.

The air is shaken by it;
The horrible monsters
Have torn asunder
All its bosom.

Now it is raining: the water
That breaks loose
And showers
Cold on the abundant

Fluctuating crops,
Wants, as it seems,
To submerge,
Wrathfully, the world.

Ferdinando Fiorillo

GOLD-HAIRED GIRL

O girl with golden hair
Who, after the sun rose,
Sang in your garden, where
There is a scent of rose,

You do not know nor care
That in my heart arose,
Through your enchanting air,
Regrets long in repose.

You take me back to a time
All cheerfulness and glee,
To a past all gold and pearl:

When my sweetheart sublime
Sang with high melody
Like you, O gold-haired girl.

Ferdinando Fiorillo

FLOWERS
To my mother and mother-in-law

Flowers in my garden were cut off, you see,
When Spring came to us full of pleasantness.
I always looked at them admiringly
And daily used to cheer them and caress.

It was a red rose and a lily white
Of greatest beauty, to be sure, and charm.
I never would have foreseen such a plight,
Nor did suspect the nature of the harm.

They were cut off, and now I am bereft
Of their sweet smell and shape so beautiful.
I'd like to see them: till I'm lifeless left
I will be desolate and sorrowful.

I would revive them even with my tear
And with my prayers and sorrowful lament,
I'd like to suffer with them, to stay near
Until my time on earth is fully spent.

Carnations, jasmines, violets still grow,
Daffodils, tulips and the tuberose;
But in my garden, ah, are wanting now
A soft white lily and a fragrant rose.

Vincenzo Foti

Note: The mother and mother-in-law of Vincenzo Foti
died on the same day: March 19, 1951.

THE LITTLE DEAD BIRD

Walking today along the lonely sea,
Upon the tender newly growing grass,
Beside some fallow clods and turfs, alas,
I saw a little bird in agony.
    He lay inert near by a rigid pole
Which propped some bare and thin electric wire.
Sure he was there to enjoy and to admire
The heavenly sun, a balm to every soul,
    When pitiless Death took hold of him with rigor,
About to start upon his wandering life,
Perhaps. I picked him up, tried to revive
Without delay, to give him even new vigor,
    So that he might resume his wonted flight,
Since I believed he still was warm and breathing;
But in my hands, that held him softly beating
The bird expired, poor thing, so neat and bright!
    What to do now? I viewed him for a while,
Thinking of what he only one hour before
Had been . . . of the short time, perhaps a score
Of days? he fought like man on sea, earth, isle.
    What to do now? to carry him with me
And eat him as Epicureans do,
Who are blind and gluttons? Gentlemen, ne'er you
Would do it, nor a man of poetry!
    Not far from me there was a heap of earth,
Thrown there by a good farmer, and some sand.
There, O my friends, the little bird did end
His secret struggle, both for food and flirt.
    Just as we are doing with our fallen brave,
After removing a small bit of soil,
I buried him, and the wild beasts to foil
I strewed with odorous flowers his lowly grave.
    Dear little bird! who knows how many times
I saw you fly on strong and rapid wings
And your eternal idyl weave and sing
Tenderly in these uncultivated climes,
    On these deserted grassy fields! Who knows
How many mornings through that windowsill
Flapping your wings you tried to reach me, still
Stretched on my bed, with closed and sleepy brows!
    Oh, you too were amid the numerous mates

Who used to fly there! For the crafty fowls
Are going in flocks and mock the wolf that howls,
Or the lone kite, or even the roving cats.
    Meanwhile your happy days are gone forever,
O little bird, so dear to human eyes!
Every dear mate of yours that chirps and flies
From now on will in vain search with his clever
    And so keen looks your lovely shape; in vain
The grass and flowers that here around will wither,
Will wait for you to come triumphant hither . . .
For you these shores are sad, and I feel pain.

Giuseppe Incalicchio

CONVOYS
During the Second World War

Set sail and brave the storm,
O ships with steely sides,
Laden by rough, patient hands
Of humble people,
By stooping, honest workers.
Set sail, and reach the shores
Of the distant land where
They suffer and await anxiously
The food they lack, and sigh . . .
The food which was destroyed
In this hellish, horrid war,
Of which the earth is tired.
O, what sad vicissitude,
Is this long, cruel war!
O, may return our peace!
Now give us ships, a proof
Of your fine, faultless gear.
Come, on, allay the ills
Of all those suffering folk.
Defy the powerful sea
Which sneers at the foe's snares.
Set sail, o convoys, full
Of goods, with fire and faith,
Steered on by skillful pilots,
Heave your sharp bows and cut
The water, o convoys,
And bring light far away;
The blessing bring of Heaven

There where they sigh and starve,
Bring peace of mind and love
To those who still believe,
Poor folks, in a better fate,
In chosen spirits' help.
You are the ornament and pride
Of an awakened nation.
You carry while you sail
Within your large, deep holds
What our wild foe destroyed . . .
O, plow the sea's expanse
Which is so dense and blue,
And brave the huge, white waves,
O, convoys, and escape
The snares of submarines,
Of those insidious wolfpacks.
You are, I know, an object
Of envy to all those who fear
The bright sunshine in the morn;
You are the rightful force
Which crushes and knocks out
The blind force of the fiend.
This is a very huge toil,
Therefor we must fight on,
On land and on deep seas;
And you, as hope's conveyance,
Bring bread and also love
To those who bleed and weep.
Bring peace to the poor folks
Who wait and crave for justice,
Not for revenge, and wait
For our arrival, so that
The minds of all, near and far,
Be united, and the hearts
May fraternize on earth.
O, plow, o sturdy ships . . .
On mooring allay the hunger
Of those who are praying for you.

                              Giuseppe Incalicchio

THE POET

Dedicated to my mother on my fifty-first birthday

I am the Poet: the ascetic entertaining
Sweet thoughts.
I sing, and my song alleviates
The rough pathway of life:
Of human nature . . .
I am the Poet: the ascetic aspiring
To numberless loves,
Which I exalt rejoicingly and arid hearts
I then make fruitful and bold
With my sweet songs.

And to the beautiful, deep mystery
I turn my vivid eye;
And as a limpid water-spout
Everywhere my song is sparkling.
As fire which burns perennially
With pure and mystic flame.
My song, suave and solemn,
I dedicate to you, O Mother!

I am the Poet, like a saint
Or prophet.
The prayer I raise is a beautiful song
To my heavenly God: the Athlete
Who moves creation . . .
I am the Poet; sharp pain
Does not harm me,
And even if bread is wanting, to my heart
Your sweet voice is enough,
O celestial Muse . . .

And mysterious peace assists me
If I gaze up at the clear sky,
From which each star benignly smiles
And the poison of human folly
Gets lost in the mud,
As man, who is only made of clay,
In vain contests every way
And every goal of the Almighty God.

I am the Poet and the ascetic
Of the beautiful only
That beautiful which you, O nature,
Make the goal of every artistic song
Shine with enchantment . . .
Only in this is my world; the rest is worthless.
If my soul
Has the sky for roof, the earth for cradle,
For pallet a beautiful meadow and its calm,
Life is rejoicing . . .

I don't want mansions and gardens,
Nor estates and vassals,
But only the fulgent daybreaks
And sunsets on mountains and valleys;
Gold I don't want, nor silver,
Nor do I want relishing dishes;
I just want in my heart a chime
Of roseate hopes . . .

I am the Poet, O Mother, and my song
Has for goal
The beautiful and sweet song of yours;
That lullaby
Sung at the cradle,
The cradle of your adored firstborn
You dreamed over it
Who knows what future? but fate
Willed him a poet and denied him
The glory of the world . . .

If a shade of glory some day
Crowns, by chance, my brow with laurel,
Remember, O Mother: the source
You were, and it is yours. I honor you
In this song which eternally from my heart
Breaks out. It is the solemn echo
Of your great, noble love, which is
Beautiful and perennial.

Giuseppe Luongo

MOMENT OF DISCOMFORT

In this delightful site,
Under my plum tree, one
Enjoys springtime today.

The sun above is bright,
But a black cloud upon
My heart descends: ay, ay!

Pietro S. Moncada

YOU LOVE ME NO MORE

You forsook me and love me no more,
Bleeding, ah, is my heart's deep sore;
The hopes I used to entertain
          Proved to be vain.

Ah, what an agony and smart
I feel inside of my sick heart!
All seems to me dead on the earth,
The moon and sun, once full of mirth.
You don't love me. When I came back
From far in vain: you chased me, alack!
But where to go now to forget?
          To a minaret?

You don't love me any more; yet, please,
You won't hate me, I hope? In peace
Then, I'll love you in phantasy:
          You're lost to me!

Ah, what an agony and smart
I feel inside of my sick heart!
All seems to me dead on the earth,
The moon and sun once full of mirth.

Stefano Moroni

SPRING SONG

Lovely Spring, return, we call;
For you my soul is waiting.
You are the season best of all;
     Friendly and warm your sun.

Meadows green and fragrant flowers,
Smile on my heart a-flowing.
My heart is looking for your bowers,
    Eager for joy and fun.

Dear little birds that sing so gay,
    In the blue sky returning;
Whispering streamlets at your play,
    I hear your siren sounds.

O my weary, exhausted heart!
    It's time to doff your sadness.
The good earth smiles at her new start
    And air with mirth resounds.

                                    Stefano Moroni

STORM

The wind howls with fury through
The green valley and the mountain,
And the thunder, roaring too,
Seems to shake the pale horizon.

Quits the peasant in that moment
In a hurry his small farm,
And runs home, poor man, afraid
Of some accidental harm.

All of nature is now blinded
By the lightning, and the rain,
From the sky all overcast,
Falls in torrents on the plain.

The wild beasts, too, are so frightened
They come out of the dark wood
And run here and there a-trembling,
Splashing in the rain and mud.

Ah, at last the storm relents,
The clouds go, the sky is blue,
And the sun, majestic now,
Reappears and shines anew.

                                    Giovanni Pisano

MEMORIAL DAY

Every grave is strewn with flowers.
Before each mound
Small groups of people kneel
To remember those
Who once had a part
In this human family, and were dragged out
By the vehemence of destiny.
From the grandeur of this evocation
Comes the strength of example
Meditated on the edge of trenches,
Where the heroes fell,
To crown with laurel and glory
Their Star-Spangled Banner,
The sacred symbol of their country.
Today the heroes sleep
In the shadow of humble crosses
Planted upon the sod,
So they may remain as watchful sentries
Of their sleep.
Memorial Day is the most sacred day
In the American people's heart,
For on this day of meditation
They exalt and purify their heroes
Who sacrificed their lives for the safety
Of the Fatherland.
On this famous, spotless date,
Worthy of history and legend,
The American people
By the most solemn celebrations
Carve their exploits
In bronze and marble
So that the glory of their fallen sons
May grow immortal.
On this memorable day
They draw their highest poetry from the solemn
Silence of graves, to make the apotheosis
Of their dauntless boys
Who are sleeping in distant cemeteries,
In the deserts of Algeria,
On the Italian Apennines,
On the fields of France,

In the valleys of Germany,
On the scorched islands of the Pacific,
On the barren Korean ridges,
Exiles in death,
Lulled by the songs of winds,
Surrounded by the fruitful light of the sun,
Watched by the golden glance of stars.

Giovanni Pisano

THE CHURCH STEEPLE

On the wide plain beneath the sloping mount
My native town lies quiet, with the tall
Old steeple of the church, which is a fount
Of prayer to fill with peace the soul.

From the few hillocks, murmuring, flow down
Clear streamlets among trees and vineyards, where
The first sweet dreams and love-songs I have known
Under the sun once brightened up the air.

But one day, when grown up to be a man,
A voice came on a sudden from overseas:
"Hello! bid farewell to the steeple, then
Come to this land to work: don't miss the chance!"

After long years I'm coming back to you,
My native town, of whom I've thought with love,
To see again the steeple and the blue
Expanse of sea, the boundless sky above.

What a delusion! Why did I come back?
For your old fascination is no more:
Wherever I turn my looks, I see, alack!
Your joy transformed into a painful sore.

Upon your square the steeple in the back
Rings now no mystic bell, not for a bit;
The people, no more cheerful, coming round,
Just look at you suspiciously, and quit.

Now you appear to me like a big ill
Person whose body has suffered many a harm;
No songs are coming from the nearby hill,
And even the air seems now to be less warm.

You too, my native town, were hit by war . . .
And the old steeple belfry chimes no more.

Vincenzo Proia

[79]

TO A CHILD

There is innocence in your eyes
As in those of an angel of paradise.
You know what human sufferings mean,
O adored child with cheerful mien.

You smile at me, your heart enjoys,
While I play with one of your toys.
When I thoughtfully look at you
My pain is vanishing like dew.

But if for an instant I go away,
You cry as if to ask me to stay.
Your anxious cry is grieving me
Because I love you too much, you see.

You are my joy, you can solace
My troubled life, and so my face
Brightens when I see you smile, content.
You only, O child, are innocent.

Vincenzo Proia

OPTIMIST

The optimist has a creed,
Which is, not to think any harm;
All that surrounds him is indeed,
"International"—city or farm.

The optimist is by nature
Serious, sober; he subscribes;
He cuts a wonderful figure,
At membership never gibes.

The optimist is an altruist,
Of children he takes care;
He practices morality, shunning mist,
Looks for knowledge everywhere.

Great men, statesmen and scientists,
Heads of nations who don't bluff,
All were excellent optimists;
Their deeds are proof enough.

Both Lincoln and Washington,
The two great nationalists,
Columbus, Marconi, and Edison,
Were, surely, all optimists.

Were it not for optimism,
The world would be bad, perverse;
We would have no more idealism
Which governs the universe.

Joseph Rosa

THE GRAIN OF WHEAT
To Rev. Herbert Johnson

A grain of wheat is a big thing,
A beautiful treasure to me,
If you put it into the soil in the spring,
Its sprouting is a thing to see.
It's the king of all the seeds:
It gives wheat in quantity
To make whole bread for men and kids
And biscuits of quality.

Even our Friend told us outright,
In a fine comparison:
"The grain of wheat has all the right
To the title of champion."

Yes, Herbert Johnson, yesterday,
Told the Optimists (no yarn)
That, if well sown, a bushel may
Fill up a good-sized barn.

Now the same thing I say, my friends:
Wheat is a wonder for men;
Because it contains the best God sends:
Flour, semolina, and bran.

I want to sing of it all the year
And repeat my hymn to all:
A grain of wheat . . . oh, it is, my dear,
Bigger than my heart . . . yet so small!

Joseph Rosa

THE BEAUTIFUL AIR

Air is essential, the very first element,
All over the world needed most;
We can't dispense with it for our development.
Though we all die, none is lost.

Air is not really a palpable thing,
Nor even a worldly object;
We don't drink or eat it, yet everything
You can find in this world is its subject.

Men and women and animals,
None of them live without air;
Plants and flowers and vegetables,
Without it exist nowhere.

Air is more useful, by my vote,
Than sun or moon or a star;
More beautiful, pressing in your throat,
Than anything near or far.

Air is the power always invoked
In all life's dangers and fears;
When stifled by fire, or by water choked,
Or snipped by the Parcae's shears . . .

Oh, how grateful we should be to Him
Who gives us pure air for our breath! . . .
As long as there's air in which to swim,
I'm not afraid even of Death.

Joseph Rosa

THE NECKLACE

On going away from you, my lady, I thought
Of giving you a necklace full of sheen,
Made of a chain which is of very thin
And real gold, all wonderfully wrought.

It is composed (around, you see, is all
Studded with charming pearls in double row)
By those my hopes which you considered low
And which I cherished in my kindled soul.

[82]

When I am far away, when you will hear
And feel the wind of sheer fatality
Blow against you invincible like a blast,

Looking at the fine necklace that I, dear,
Gave you, being enamored, you will be
Full of remorse and longing for the past.

Nando Rossi

OATH

I write to you for the last time today,
Having your shape before my fantasy;
But I think also of the lies one day
You used by thousands, sweetheart, to tell me.

I know . . . that you did not behave too well,
That you have been a liar, a "demirep";
You're changing as the wind, at every step,
Whene'er you see a man who looks at you.

You have a heart inclined to please all men:
You can't refuse, so much you like to flirt;
Your play is such that "ace wins even the shirt";
You know all tricks . . . don't say it is not true!

As for me, well, I'm through; and I am glad.
Don't call me, since you are not worthy of me.
I swore, and took my oath upon a sad
Lone grave, so it may last eternally.

Nando Rossi

I AM IMMENSELY RICH

Oh, I am rich, immensely rich, you see . . .
If I were richer I would simply die;
And I will tell you now the reason why
Richer than that I really could not be.

Master of towns and castles I am not;
I do not go for money, a base thing;
I hate all stingy men and those who sing
Happy for all the jewels they have got.

[83]

I am immensely rich! I say it aloud.
The bread I eat I'm earning by my sweat;
My children all, and my dear, gentle mate
Are all my treasure, and of them I'm proud.

For me, they are indeed the real wealth,
With which no other can on earth compare:
Love and devotion, joy and hope, the rare
Essence of my sweet dreams, beauty and health.

I rightfully feel rich, oh, very rich
With my good wife and children all near by.
And I repeat a hundred times that I
Am rich, oh, very rich, nay, over-rich.

Sinibaldo Rovito

ODE TO THE SUN

O Sun, illuminating
The dwellings of the air,
Where do you draw your magic,
Supernal splendor? where?

Oh, tell me, for what wonder
You keep in balance true
Through space, the planets turning
In orbits so round you?

Eager to solve that mystery,
Man, sketching plans and schemes,
A thousand calculations,
Hypotheses and whims,

Decided to name faculae,
Granule and chromosphere
The embers now maintaining,
Coruscant, your wide sphere;

And he concluded also
That, by Our Lord's decree,
You are appointed arbiter
Of planets' land and sea.

However, what is proving
This odd word string of mine?
For me enough—to praise you,
O marvelous Sun divine!—

To know that from your igneous,
Indefinite mass in strife,
Upon the earth you lavish
All light, all heat, all life.

Nicola Testi

PESSIMISTIC OBSERVATION

The teacher of psychology
Thus was explaining to his students:
"Among the basic laws on which
The steady change of man's existence
Becomes eternal
The one, excelling all others
For size and power,
Is that mysterious one of love,
By Schopenhauer called
'The genius of species,'
And without which . . ."
"Oh, without which," dares to remark
A voice facetious from the class,
"The asylums for the insane would be less crowded,
And the grave-diggers far less busy."

Nicola Testi

MEETING

Since the bright moment when we chanced to meet,
A longing irresistible took hold of me,
To have you with me; whisper: "O my sweet,
I love you!—and it will not let me be.
The fascination of your lovely face
Makes my heart eager for a friendly glance—
But am I really worthy of that grace?
Only the hope that someday you may chance
To tell me just one word of love and cheer
Keeps up the vital throbbing in my veins,
One little word—O beautiful and dear!
Otherwise nothing of my heart remains.

John Tatty

[85]

III

ORIGINAL ENGLISH POEMS
OF ITALO-AMERICAN POETS

ENTICING LULLABY

Please, go to sleep, my dear little child!
Sleep gives you health and makes you grow bright.
Fair is the weather, the air is mild.
I am sure you will have a wonderful night.

Please, fall asleep, O sweetheart of mine;
I hope you will dream of flowers galore,
Dream too of toys, of angels divine
Who'll keep for you all of the graces in store.

Dream about things which all will bring joy.
Light for your mind and food for your soul—
The things so happy which God would enjoy
To have for Himself, to have for our goal.

Dream about Heaven, Christ on the throne
Waiting for us to receive His embrace.
Sleep, my sweet child, you are not alone:
We are with you with smiles on our face.

Darling, think only of beautiful things;
Let's kiss good night, now you have to rest.
Listen! I hear a soft voice that sings
Sweet songs for you that all are the best.

Relax, little one, let me hold your dear hand:
I'll stay here with you, at your side I will be.
Some day, I hope, you'll perhaps understand
What my care for you means . . . what you mean to me.

Now, go to sleep, because from the sky
God will come down to watch over you,
Angels will sing a sweet lullaby;
So, till tomorrow, my dear one, adieu!

John J. Alifano

THOU LINGERING THOUGHT

Thou, love and life inspiring, thou
Lingering thought of mine! Wilt thou
Wait for me in vain? Wilt thou encourage
My weary and waiting soul to bliss, and
With a futile strain? or wilt thou,
Becoming weary of waiting, lose sight of me?

Wilt thou, my love-inspiring soul and
Mind, wilt thou have me linger for a while,
Atone this momentary task of mine, and then
Have me pass to yonder fields, to realms
Infinite and unknown, to a state of earthly
Happiness and bliss, for me also to leave
My footprints on the "Sands of Time?"

Wilt thou have me tarry
For another while, to fulfill my
Momentary halt, and then give me
Back my life's longing; and then
Fulfill my life's ambition of duty and trust?

Wilt thou? Wilt thou? Then,
I'll wait! But wilt thou then grant
Me time to complete the longing of
My heart's desire? Wilt thou then
Grant me time, only time, ere I, too,
Pass behind the veil, in yonder space?

Vincent D. Calenda

I THINK AND PONDER

Ah, me! I think and ponder
Every moment of my life—all my life,
Moments wherein I appear
To all the world at rest,—I think and ponder.

Yet fortunate that it is so,
For it was just thus I achieved
All that I have and I possess;
All that I know—that I possess.

[90]

The spare, wasted moments so used
Make great men great,—not college
Courses or degrees alone, but spare
Moments, naturally employed, these make them great.

I think and ponder every moment
Of my life, my poor, dear life;
Just when everybody thinks me
At rest, I think and ponder.

But I am happy that it
Should be so, for it is just thus
That I philosophize, and so
Solve many problems of life.

I think and ponder every
Moment of my life, my poor, dear life;
While home longing, or in my library,
Or in the midst of crowded Broadway
In the courtroom or corridor or elsewhere—

Ah, me! I think and ponder
Every moment of my life.

Vincent D. Calenda

THE GOLDEN CITY

Workers, look! Enjoy this vision
of the Golden City! Do!
Your good work for man's ascension
now is putting it in view.

Those who sought it through the ages
only saw it in their dreams,
but the Dream's realization
now is near, and, lo! it gleams . . .

This the City be of Justice,
of which Prophets spoke and Seers,
This the City be of Freedom
That shall wipe off wrongs and tears.

Workers, only through your union
you can make this City be.

Brotherhood be its foundation,
which does mean Humanity.

See to it now that no longer
exploitation shall have worth,
that the need of man's redemption
shall unite all men on earth.

Hate, oppression, prejudices,
tyranny and servitude,
must at last all be destroyed
for Humanity's real good.

All our minds and hands uniting,
let's surround the City Blest.
Love, the most sacred Ideal,
shall triumph in every breast.

Yes, this wonder of all ages
shall destroy every vile chain,
while Love shall bind all the Nations . . .
Peace on earth! Good will to men! . . .

Antonino Crivello

TO OUR LORDS

You are not made of different stuff.
Your bones and flesh will rot within this earth.
You too will mingle with the dust and stones
and as a fertilizer you'll have worth.

In vain you pose as God's selected ones . . .
Your crimes and faults atrocities give forth,
but you shall tumble down from your high thrones.
There's no fleeing to East, West, South, or North!

Your pride, your power, your gold cannot stop death.
Why do you spill men's blood and hoard and steal?
What good are riches after the last breath?

We're not eternal, but you grab and . . . save! . . .
For death? Oh, with the devil make your deal! . . .
But can you take a thing into the grave?

Antonino Crivello

A HYMN TO THE NIGHT

O Night, blessed may you be
for the quietness
that with you falls
over all things
created.
And blessed may you be
for the peace
and the contentment
that you bring
to all those
who honestly
devote themselves
to their daily
toil
and fraternally
love one another.

And blessed may you be
for the revelation
of the mysterious
Universe,
that, through
the infinity
of your clear
heaven, to us
you disclose.

And blessed may you be
for the light of the stars
and for that of the moon
and for that of the firefly
in June.

And blessed may you be
for all the mysterious
voices
that through the deep
stillness
of the forests
you bring to our ears,
and for the monotonous
songs

of the crickets
in the fields
and for the chatting
murmur
of the water
that bubbling
falls
in the fount.

And blessed may you be
for the aroma
that emanates
from the freshly
cut grass,
and for the acute
perfume of the lilies
and for that
of the roses
and for that
immensely
acute,
of the tuberoses;
and for the perfumes
of all flowers
and all plants
and all herbs
and all verbenas,
that you, through your quietness,
mysteriously
force out of my garden
and to my
nostrils
make more sensitive
and suave.

And blessed may you be
for the dew,
the food divine
on which
the singer of the sun,
the daughter of the soil,
    sacred to Apollo,
    cicada,
    feeds.

But, blessed may you be
above all
for the silence
that through
my room
you diffuse,
for in this
I find,
in my solitude,
the lover of my dreams
of the infinite,
inexhaustible
accents:
Thalia,
and while
others sleep,
in her company
dreamingly
I live on poetry,
O night, blessed may you be!

Giuseppe Luongo

TO MY NATIVE LAND

This is my native land! Along the road
Where Hercules once drove his cattle through,
Tall red geraniums boldly face the sun,
In fervid challenge to the ocean's blue.
Over the bridge that once great Caesar built,
A shepherd crosses with his humble herd—
I stop the car to give him right of way,
And neither one of us dares speak one word.

No doubt the shepherd thinks me rich and proud—
(I've turned away my face to hide my tears . . .)
He can not guess that I am leaning back
To touch with trembling hands the dust of years.

Rosa Zagnoni Marinoni

ANOTHER THRONE FOR THE PRINCE OF PEACE

Along the muddy road to Bethlehem,
The least and lost Judean town,
Wind up at last their weary journey
The travellers of regal noun.

[95]

Alert are the man's eyes and muscles,
   And deep concern his mind doth hold,
   For there expectant virgin mother
   Close by him follows, tired and cold.

Descendants all of kingly David,
   Their hearts protect the royal heir—
   The Prince of Peace, who comes to govern
   Upon the throne of his Forbear.

But there's no throne, no crown, no scepter
   Awaiting this belated King;
   The country's chained by foreign fetters,
   And cities with rebellion ring;

There is no court, no army standing
   This ruler to welcome and greet,
   No pomp, no servants, and no ministers
   Are there the Sovereign Lord to fete.

And so, in loving condescension,
   Another throne the Prince will find:
   It'll be the heart of every human
   Where God's love lives for all mankind.

                    P. S. Moncada

THE BUILDER

"What I am building here
Little by little, lonely,
With the pure ardor of an ancient Roman
Is something uncommon."
   I asked him curious: "A monument?
A temple all shining with gold?
A steely tower which every wind
Defies? an immense forum?"
   The man answered: "What
You named are things that come to nothing
Under the horrible scourge of time:
I'm doing a thing whose firmness and renown
Increase with time."
"Say, what? High pillars?"
"No, with my heart which bleeds and yet loves
I throw a great bridge of hymns toward the stars."

                    Rodolfo Pucelli

THE POET TODAY

There is no hope, no cure-all any more:
All things are upside down upon the earth.
The poet who was heard with joy and worth
And welcome seems today to be a bore.

Time was in every place men praised his lore,
Both young and old; approval knew no dearth.
The farmerettes, light-hearted, full of mirth,
Intoned his songs to ease an inward sore.

Now for his candid rhymes nobody cares;
Instead, uncaring men speak only ill
Of him as if he were of lower race.

Police encountering him unawares
Suspect he only wants to rob or kill,
Then grin and look him sternly in the face.

Rodolfo Pucelli

THE MOTH OF THOUGHT

Thus the wee moth of thought
Pierces my vivid brain,
That seems to turn a gimlet
Always, with might and main.

If I could drive him out!
But I am his poor slave
And will be forced to take him
With me into the grave!

How wild are his attacks!
How wrathfully he bores
At some whimsical hour!

My brain already cracks . . .
My soul, however, adores
And cherishes his power.

Rodolfo Pucelli

THE HAPPY WREN

How cheerful and how happy, O wren,
Little amid the little birds,
You seem in your low hedges, when
You skip and fill the air with chirps.

I saw you while I walked at dawn,
Or rather when the sun of God
Rose on the hill, lighting the lawn:
And stopped to watch you from the road.

You skipped and stopped and skipped anew
In search of what I could not guess:
Maybe 'twas an insect that flew,
A creeping worm, good for your mess.

Maybe 'twas only gleam and glory,
Fresh air, the colored flowers' scent;
Maybe 'twas love (a very old story!)
That pushed you on with merriment.

O little bird, I don't care much
To know which reason drove you on:
You were so charming, you were such
A lovely creature, that a moan

Came from my heart, and thus I said:
—Oh if I were not a poor man,
As I am, but a wren instead!
I would be simply happy then!

Rodolfo Pucelli

TO FLORIO VITULLO
After reading his posthumous poems

I've heard the voice of many poets, yet
I never heard an echo of your song
Before you died. In sweet Italian tongue
By now you've made yourself undying, great.

Your dear and faithful wife, with eyes still wet,
Religiously picked up your poems among
Your scattered papers, not to do any wrong
To you, who were so much with cares beset.

[98]

A book came out so full of beautiful lines
That many were surprised and said:"Egad,
He was a poet and could have been well known."

My good Vitullo, how my heart now pines
For your departure, since I never had
The joy to meet you, nor to see your town!

Rodolfo Pucelli

TO DOLEFUL AQUILEIA

If you were not, o noble Aquileia,
So desolate and deprived
Of authority, strength and fortune,
But still would come to you,
Through the lagoon, ships loaded with
Merchandise bought in Orient;
If you were happy
And still inhabited by those people
Who were clad in sumptuous purple:
Oh, you wouldn't have let me go
Far in the world like an adventurer,
I am quite sure of that,
But you would have offered me
A hut, a humble little house,
So that I might remain
With you and sing a hymn in your behalf.
Oh, how glad would I have been,
Aquileia, to find myself
There near the house where I was born,
At a few steps from the place where the Capitol
Shone with marbles and mosaics!
But nothing remains today of you,
That once were the Second Rome.
Only from your profound solitude
Are jutting out the remains
of your famous haven,
The marble tombs, some broken cippus,
A plinth, a capital,
A crooked tripod,
A mutilated statue
Of Caesar or of fatuous
Pagan divinity.

Now I am living in a land far away
From your fertile land where the wheat
Oscillates lightly in the wind
And the brisk linnets
Sing cheerfully, ignorant of your fate;
And I see no more your mild and terse
Rivulets, murmuring amid Roman tombs
And cinerary urns.
Nor the Natissa which silently flows
As in its glorious days,
But among vast morasses and shadowy meadows.
Often from my tired eyes
Glides down a tear because
Always will be vain my lively wish
To live with you and to sing
Your glories, sitting under an elm tree,
A willow or a tall poplar
Or near a pleasant row of vine.

Aquileia, I would like to exalt you
Like Paulin, your most faithful and dear son,
But I am living here
Among the noises and I feel sometimes
As one who loses all his strength of mind.
Yet to my heart you are
Like a gem and you glitter
Like an ethereal star, and almost every day
I return to you
On the swift wings of my faithful thought,
O my doleful native town
Abandoned on the green plains
Of the beautiful Friul, wrapt in the large veil
Of a deep melancholy,
Especially when through the sky
Is vanishing the echo of your bells
And in the vast silence that follows
Is heard a croaking of frogs
And the barking of a dog.

Rodolfo Pucelli

THE DAY I MET YOU

The day I met you, dear,
  Was the culminating point of my ambition!
Till then my heart was sad,
  Low was my spirit's condition.

You dispersed my frightful darkness,
  A life of storm and strife;
You brought me joys unknown,
  An oasis of beauty and of life.

Every sorrow you dispelled
  With your love, incomparable and true.
You put an end to all my griefs,
  My heart found heaven in you!

Only love can work miracles
  And your love did it to me!
You wiped out all my tears,
  You chased all my torment of yesterday!

The day I met you, dear,
  Was really a blessed day!
I now enjoy life's wealth:
  Your love, and the lofty things you say!

The day I met you, dear,
  Was the complement of all my dream!
'Twas the only desire I've ever coveted,
  Love, lo! is the wealth supreme!

Yes! the day I met you, dear,
  God entered into me!
As you entered the same as He,
  Holy things now I feel and see!

Whoever this divine touch wants to feel
  And see things sweet and fair,
Love only he should implore
  As I did in my long prayer!

Frank Spadola

[101]

IT'S WONDERFUL TO BE IN LOVE

It's wonderful to be in love,
　It's heaven, this is true.
But it all depends on whom we love;
　This has a lot to do.

Love can only be wonderful
　If one loves a noble soul!
Only then we can feel true ecstasy
　And say we've reached the goal.

If one loved an unworthy person,
　What true joys could it bring?
Love would cease to be wonderful,
　Shame it would bring and sting.

But I know whom I'm loving . . .
　From her come sublime feelings!
In her I find honor, elation;
　She soars above all things!

Loving, loving a worthy one
　Is divine, if that one is like mine!
Loving is carrying God with us
　And lasting the space of time!

Frank Spadola

THE GREAT POWER!

Who gives us words and sound
For our daily enterprise?
And who lends us wings from the ground
Our ideas may loftily arise?

Who lifts us unto the sky
And beautifies our daily life?
There's only one power, you and I
Know, and for it we gladly strive.

Through this power, all we achieve:
Prestige and wealth and fame;
Through this power, all we receive:
Honor, immortal name.

And you know of what power I talk,
And what beauty moves our heart!
Love! is that power that makes us walk,
Live and create great works of Art!

Love is that only power which inspires
With lofty sentiments and deeds;
Love unites mankind in one desire
To banish hatred, and aid others' needs.

I love all, the rich and the poor,
The negro, white, and the yellow;
I love all, whoever taps at my door.
All l help, as I have and know.

Above all, God I love, my supreme!
He who gave me this impulse,
He who made me realize my dream
In a world where love ceased to pulse.

O Love, O sweetness divine,
Never abandon me!
Leave me to love all, though not worthy of thine,
Leave me to love the one worthy of thee!

Frank Spadola

YOU LEAVE . . .

You leave,
But I don't know how long I'll live
After you're gone away.

You leave,
But I don't know how I could weave
Another romance
After you and I
Built one so high.
We were as if in heaven
Amidst music and song,
Happy to each other to belong.

You leave,
But you know I will always grieve
Till you come back again.

You leave,
But, darling, how can I believe
That you're far away?
I feel you're near me
Smiling tenderly.
I hear you always say:
You see, I'm not away,
Yet, dear, the truth is there.

You leave,
But without you, dear, how can I live
Just with your memory?

How can I live?

Frank Spadola

SOMETHING OF THE PAST

We used to join a summer day
    Around a walnut tree,
The walnut tree beside the way,
    Far off beyond the sea!

We laughed, we danced, we had much fun,
    And life seemed then so fair!
I am, alas, the only one
    Who's living, far from there.
            . . .
Life now has been too long for me;
    My heart fails in my breast.
I see beside another tree,
    The tree that gives me rest!

Green cypress, then, I wish thy shade,
    Where I shall have my grave;
I wish some flowers that won't fade;
    My sea will send her wave.

Joseph Rizzo Taranletti

FRANCESCA

She was born in Florence,
The city of culture and art,
The home of Michelangelo,
Near the Arno River.

Having married a great statesman,
Whom she helped reach a high goal,
With her charm and her work
She became First Lady of the State.

She came back from abroad,
After visiting the land of her birth,
Which she loves like America
And can never forget.

Wearing a bright-colored Sardinian costume,
With a Florentine cape,
And wooden soled sandals on her feet,
She went lecturing on Italian art.

Always helping the poor
And the people in distress,
She is a model of a lady
To look upon.

John Tatty

BIOGRAPHICAL NOTES

Bruno Agazzi was born in Torino, where he now resides. He is a journalist, poet, and writer; active and very well known.

Dr. John J. Alifano was born in Lioni. He came to the United States as a boy, started studying in English, went to college. Well known as a physician and surgeon, he writes poetry in both languages. His recent book, *Verso l'Aurora*, is a true specimen of his skill as a poet. He lives in Springfield, Massachusetts.

Claudio Allori is famous in Italy. He has written numerous books in prose and verse; has won first prize in poetry contests.

Augusto Arrigoni, publicist, writer, and poet; born 1923, is already among the best young poets.

Michelangelo Mazzeo Barmich, born in Barcellona, province of Messina, in 1921. He published *I Poemi del Bacio,* also a book for children and many poems. He lives in Trivero (Vercelli).

Efrem Bartoletti, born in 1869 in Costacciaro (Umbria). At the age of twenty, he landed in the United States, where he worked in coal mines in Scranton, Pennsylavania. He wrote *Nostalgie Proletarie* and many lengthy poems in which he defends needy workers, despises tyrants.

Prof. Francesco Berloco, born in Altamura, province of Bari, lives in Palermo. He has won literary contests. Noteworthy is his *Triptych.*

Carlo Bianco, writer, critic, and poet, resides in Cervinara. He teaches Italian language and literature. He has published several works, notable for fine prose, vast thoughts, and keen mind.

Alvaro Bongi, a poet of renown, dramatizes, reveals the desolate desperation of present-day Italy. He is a serious critic; resides in Florence.

Plinio Bulleri, born in Ponte Buggianese (Pistoia). His poems are sincere, fluent, plain. His language is always correct. He has published successfully a few short books of poetry. Resident of Cicero, Illinois.

Nino Caradonna is one of the most admired poets among Italo-Americans. In Italy his name is known almost anywhere. Printer and occasionally publisher, he is very active. Books: *Sogni e Faville, Gridi dell'Anima, E l'Uomo Pensa, I Canti di un Raggio do Sole, etc.* He was born in Alcamo, Sicily. A deep thinker, but often uncertain and tormented by doubts.

Aldo Capasso is a poet of strong interior analysis; very sensitive. His poetry is human, but full of anxiety and dissatisfaction. He is one of the best poets and critics. Born in Venice in 1909. Resides in Altare (Savona).

Antonio Cappa, founder-director of the Italian Notarial School, is a well known poet. Depicts nature; is always clear, delicate, and pleasant.

Rolando Certa, one of the youngest Italian poets (born 1931 in Palermo). He published *Pallido Mondo,* a book of verse, in 1953. Favorably reviewed.

Roberto Cervo was born at Caiazzo (Caserta), September 29, 1921. Founder of *Movimento Esistenziale Spiritualista Poetico Italiano.* He has written much. His book of poetry, *Esistenzia Supina,* has increased his renown in Italy and abroad. He resides in Bergamo; editor of *La Nuova Italia Letteraria,* one of the most beautiful Italian magazines. His wonderful long poem, *Polesine Amaro,* was translated into English by Rodolfo Pucelli. A new bilingual edition is in press.

Riccardo Cordiferro (pseudonym of Alessandro Sisca) has been the most popular Italian-American poet. He was born in Calabria in 1875, died in New York in 1940. He was editor of *La Follia di New York.* He wrote many books of poetry and drama.

Antonio Crivello, born in Palermo, is today a well known poet of the working class. He has written and published poems by hundreds in both languages, yet nothing in book form. He is manager of a Labor Union Local in Newark, New Jersey. His poems, especially those in Italian, should be collected and published as soon as possible; they have pith and meaning.

Antonio J. Daraio, born in Tricarico, Italy, came to the United States while young. He is a chiropractor, but has a real-estate business. He has written many songs and lyrics. No book published, but he hopes to have his poems in book form soon.

Scipio di Dario came to the United States while young. He works as a salesman. His wife, highly educated, is a piano teacher. They own a home in the Bronx, New York. Di Dario has written poems and songs in Italian, some of which he published in the *Follia....*

Dr. Giuseppe di Gioia is active in real estate near Bayshore, Long Island. He writes wonderfully in both languages, and is the fortunate author of novels, comedies, and dramas in English and of fine lyrics in Italian. He prefers modern form; that is, un-rhymed, but with deep thought and reasoning.

Salvatore di Leo is an outstanding Sicilian poet. He has also written important songs in Italian, set to music by V. de Crescenzo. He is perfect in form, especially when he writes sonnets. Author of some interesting books of poetry in Sicilian dialect. He lives in Brooklyn, New York.

Luigi Fiorentino, born in Mazara del Vallo (Sicily), February 13, 1913, resides in Siena; editor of *Ausonia* and author of *Basalto*. Leader of "Ausonism", an appreciated, logical, literary current. He is one of the best Italian poets. His works have been translated into many languages, and he enjoys a wide renown.

Ferdinando Fiorillo is a painter. His poems are almost all descriptive, but a few are also of love and full of sentiment. He loves nature and likes details. One of the best poets in the Italian language in the United States.

Lionello Fiumi, born in Roverchiara (Verona) in 1894. He lived in Paris for fifteen years where he was called "Literary Ambassador." Published *Anthology of Italian Poetry,* etc. Wrote much in prose. Critic. Among his works: *Mussole, Esistere nell'Oggi, Sul Cuore l'Ombra.* He is placed first after D'Annunzio.

Vincenzo Foti, born in Salice (Reggio Calabria), came to the United States very young. Likes poetry and has written some sentimental poems, which are read with pleasure. He is running a food store in Elizabeth, New Jersey. He has never published in book form.

Pino Giacopelli. Lieutenant Sixth Regiment, "Aosta," Palermo. A promising young poet.

Arturo Giovannitti is the most famous poet of the working class. In 1912 he was innocently imprisoned, and while in jail wrote one of his best English poems, "The Walker." He has written also for the stage. In Italian, he published *Parole e Sangue* in 1938, issued by the Labor Press. In Italy he enjoyed a classical education. He was born in Ripabottoni (Compobasso) in 1884.

Eugenio Gnecchi is a writer of renown, residing in Locatello Imagna, (Bergamo), where he founded a handicraft school. Former editor of *L'Italia nell' Arte.* He has written impressive philosophic essays.

Francesco Greco was born in Savelli (Catanzaro) in 1898. He attended only elementary school, but was helped by his inborn talent. He came to the United States in 1923, worked as a carpenter, then in the real-estate business. As a poet he emerges from the crowd. He has published nothing in book form.

Pietro Greco came to this country in 1904. He was born in S. Andrea Jonico (Catanzaro) in 1889. His first book was *Fremiti. Alba e Tramonto,* a large collection of classical poems, was issued in 1947.

Giuseppe Incalicchio, born in Fondi, came to the United States at an early age. He is a very much esteemed poet, classic, romantic, and especially a lover of nature. He likes to write panegyrics also. Has published three books of verse, all very good, especially *Odi Fondane.*

Giuseppe Luongo was born in S. Angelo Fasanella. A real poet, he is refined in style. Deep feeling, religious, human, good-natured. He has published *Idilli e Canzoni* and *Fatti e Visioni,* both praiseworthy. He writes also in English.

Severina Magni, one of the best Italo-American poets, was born in 1897 in Lucca, Tuscany. In the United States since 1921, she had a hard life manufacturing and embroidering flags. Her first and only book of verse, *Luci Lontane,* is precious. She felt nature, love, beauty deeply. She died in Detroit, Michigan, May 30, 1954.

Rosa Zagnoni Marinoni, born in Bologna, came to the United States as a little child. She is known as the Poet Laureate of Arkansas. Delivers speeches on the radio. She writes with deep feeling.

Antonio Manuppelli, born in 1902. Writer, publicist, poet. Very able writer of short stories. His recent book, *Ceneri alla sua Terra,* was a big success. He resides in Bovino (Foggia). A very skillful writer and poet.

Carmine Manzi, editor of *Fiorisce un Cenacolo.* Founder of Academy of Paestum. His poetry is simple and musical, almost naive. He resides near Salerno.

Guido Massarelli, editor of *Il Pungolo Verde* of Campobasso. Excellent reviewer, encourages young writers. He has written some good, human poems.

Salvatore Maturanzo lives in Naples. Author of critical essays, his poetry is fine, sincere, between classic and modern; his prose is elegant. He has written some fine novels.

Rev. Pietro S. Moncada is an excellent orator and a very good poet in both languages. Founder of an orphanage in Pachino (Sicily) his native town. He has published a book of poems, *Primavera,* which also contains a long poem full of humor. He resides in Newburgh, New York.

Stefano Moroni was born in Cori, near Rome. A Canadian soldier in the First World War. He published *Echi,* a book of poetry among the best. He has a strong bent for poetry, but his business takes almost all of his time.

Angiolo Orvieto is a great, lovable poet of the last generation. Author of several famous books of poetry. He lives in Florence, aged and with his memories. He is the best friend and warm supporter of Rodolfo Pucelli, to whom he wrote a fine poem in June, 1954.

E. C. Pedrocco, a very sensitive poet. Her poems are uncommonly fine and well written, inspired. She has written and published a great deal; contributes to numerous magazines. She lives near Udine.

Giovanni Pisano (pseudonym, *Italo Limbara*) was born near Sassari (Sardegna) in 1900. He has written many poems, songs set to music and short lyrics. He follows the classical school.

Vincenzo Proia, born in Alcamo (Sicily), came to the United States young. He has written many short stories; is an idealist and has had some bad experiences in life. Recently he published *Storia della mia vita* a delightful humorous book of verse. An accountant, he owns a barbershop in New York City.

Prof. Rodolfo Pucelli was born in Aquileia (Gorizia), March 15, 1885, and came to the United States in 1928. He is master of the principal languages of Europe and America. A well known poet and polyglot, critic, translator, and interpreter. He has published sixteen books of poetry and written in several languages. Editor of weeklies, and now of *Il Compasso,* a magazine of literature and arts. He has worked hard (during 1944-1952 six long pamphlets) to maintain peace among the peoples.

Joseph Rosa was born in Avigliano, Italy. Editor of a fashion magazine. Excellent poet in dialect; humorist. Also he writes pretty well in Italian. He is eighty years old and still writes witty poems.

Nando Rossi, pseudonym of one of the best poets in Neapolitan dialect. His real name is Ferdinando Papa. Youthful, friendly, affectionate, witty; a fine fellow. His poems, both in dialect and Italian, are appreciated by all. He is employed in the administration of *Il Progresso Italo-Americano,* New York. He is a real poet in character and behaviour as well.

Gino Rovida, who resides in Rome, wrote *Finestre Lontane* and *Aretusa e la Muraglia,* poems, novels, biographies, two books for boys, etc. He prefers free verse.

Sinibaldo Rovito lives in Shamokin, Ohio. He has written a number of poems, some of which have appeared in the *Follia* of New York. A man faithful to tradition, to his family, and his native land. A true American citizen. As a poet he is esteemed by many.

Umberto Saba, born in Trieste in 1883. He has published several books of poetry, the most discussed of which is *Il Canzoniere* (1945). He follows no school; is sentimental, lyrically inspired. One of the most esteemed poets in Italy.

Frank Spadola, born in Baragiano (Italy), came to America when he was sixteen. In Italy he won a diploma as an accountant, but in the United States he started as a barber. He wrote a number of love poems, especially in English. A very sensitive and human poet, he exalts pure love. No books published as yet; he contributes to magazines.

Anna Maria Stocchino, a professor of Italian in Rome. She has published many fine lyrical poems. Rather sad, as almost all young Italian poets are today.

Prof. Joseph Rizzo Taranletti was born in Philadelphia, Pennsylvania, where his father was a physician and pharmacist. He went to Italy while young and studied in the Lyceum of Messina, and taught there for thirty years. He still lives in Messina. He is now about seventy years old, likes classic form, and his poems are reminiscent of our best English poets.

John Tatty was born in Priverno, a province of Littoria. He has been active as director of a radio station and of the Mazzini Society in Hartford, Connecticut. He has written some good poems in both languages, but nothing in book form.

Geppo Tedeschi is known for his short poems, incisive and clear. He likes nature and all humble creatures. Nobody can imitate him. Resides near Reggio Calabria.

Nicola Testi, born in San Severo (Foggia), came to the United States at the age of twenty. He studied mechanics. His poems are so original his style cannot be mistaken, yet at times they are somewhat obscure. Through study he has improved greatly. His first book, *Stonature,* was published in 1939. Another book of poetry, *Arpe, mandole e pifferi,* came out in 1954, in Milan, Italy.

Giuseppe Trucco is "the poet of sentiment," as Roberto Cervo defines him. He has published *Quadernidi Poesia,* a magazine for poets exclusively. He resides in Catania, Sicily.

Sandro Venturini is editor of *Centro Studi Critici, Mogliano Vito* (Treviso). Critic and poet.

Giuseppe Villaroel was born in Catania, Sicily, October 16, 1869. He has published eight books of poetry since 1910. In 1951 a selection of his poems was issued under the title *L'Uomo e Dio*. His verse is musical, imaginative, and often fascinating.

Florio Vitullo, born in Bomba, Italy, in 1881, was a real poet. He lived almost unknown, running a food store in Utica, New York. After his death (1944) his good wife collected his poems. His book, *Luci e Ombre,* was read with surprise and admiration.

Dante Volpintesta, a young poet of the present generation, has gone through sad experiences. He aims at regeneration of the world, so every man can live and work in peace.

Carlo Weidlich likes the classic form. His style is terse, and he is very active. Author of anthologies, he has made praiseworthy translations from German writers. He resides in Palermo.

Armando Zamboni is a well-known poet and critic, whose work has been translated into several languages. "Sweetness" was translated by Lionello Fiumi into French.

INDEX BY AUTHORS

INDEX BY TITLES